at my pace

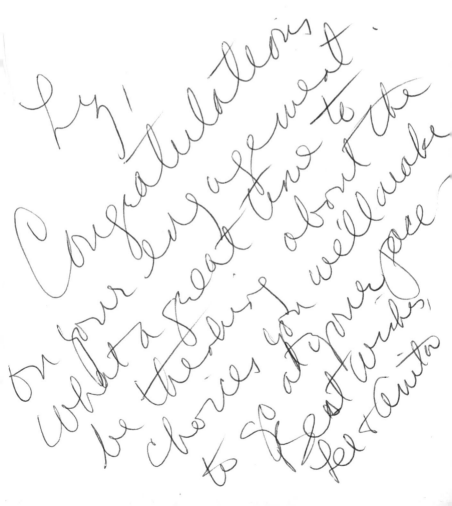

at my pace

Ordinary Women Tell
Their Extraordinary Stories

Collected and Edited by Jill Ebstein

at my pace

FIRST EDITION, 2015

ISBN: 978-0-9962674-0-3
eBook ISBN: 978-0-9962674-1-0

To Rosyne and Roz
My Mother and Mother-in-law
Two titans who paved the way

Table of Contents

III. Women in Their 70s and 80s

Introduction

Jill Ebstein

So what exactly is *At My Pace* and why?

At My Pace is a collection of essays that seeks to expand the conversation about the various ways we, as women, craft our individual journeys. For some, riding the autobahn full speed is natural and fulfilling. For others, the ride is more tortuous, full of twists and turns, yield signs, and rest stops. Both routes have much to recommend them, but we have celebrated the speedsters far more in recent years. This book focuses on women whose journeys have often been uneven, who have not only "leaned in" (to borrow a phrase from Sheryl Sandberg) but who have also leaned out and sideways.

Someone described this pool of women as "the Dove group." A while ago, Dove soap launched commercials that featured full figure women as opposed to the more typical ultra-lean models. Dove won praise for expanding their concept of beauty. The analogy is good. The women in these pages are ordinary extraordinary women who have not made headline news. They are not the models we often admire in today's glamorous, fast-paced media-hyped environment. They are models though of a different sort—strong, intuitive, and thoughtful in how they engage their world. "Inspirational" is the first word I immediately jump to when asked about these women.

Which brings me to the point of this book: My hope is that reading these stories will inspire women to conceive of more options about how they do life. I think back to when I've experienced my own version of "beat the clock." Can I get to the grocery store and back in thirty minutes, finish writing the report in time for the call, and walk the dog after I get the chicken in the oven? It can be dizzying, and, to quote a famous poet, I often felt that I was "measuring out my life in coffee spoons."[1] Maybe reading these women's stories will help alter the game from "beat the clock" to "enjoy the view."

I also have a second goal for *At My Pace*. Beyond being inspirational, I hope the essays will provide a perspective that helps us to judge ourselves and others less harshly. I have been part of way too many conversations where we challenge both the professionally ambitious and the women who are optimizing on other aspects of their life—balance, family time, community involvement, pursing an intense hobby, or maybe just "living in the present." What would it be like if we made acceptance the norm? Just maybe we can embrace the range of choices that exist, and find our own internal peace. And, just maybe, these essays can let open a crack of light where we ask, "Why not?" when we imagine some alternative path for our lives.

---

1 Eliot, T.S. "The Love Song of J. Alrfred Prufrock."

The Process

As I shared my idea for the book with friends, names started to pop up everywhere. Some were people I knew and others were referred to me by virtue of their range of experience, resilience, or unique perspective. My best friend in college was a fine artist, turned lawyer, who also loves to write. What would she have to say? (Nancy Strehlow's "Zigs and Zags and Floor-Drops"). A colleague I had worked with years ago suggested two women. One was her sister (Susana Fonticoba, "Wild Cat Mountain Revisited") who was widowed at an early age and led a remarkable path back, raising two young children and, out of necessity, starting her own business. Another was a graphic designer whose life came unraveled in the dot com bust and used ingenuity, humor and strength to do a reset (Sandy Gregory, "A Few Minor Repairs"). And so began the process. I was off to the races.

In my conversations with these women, I asked a lot of questions. Did they have an ah-ha moment? Is there a personal story that describes their essence? Was there a lesson learned that they could pass along? What do they see ahead? What did they or will they need to overcome? And by the way, can all this be shared in one pithy one thousand-word piece? It was a tall order and a collaborative process. It is far easier being on the outside and helping describe someone else's trajectory, than doing it for yourself. Hence my piece is called "Take 2", as I failed in my first attempt, which was long and dispersive. The most impressive aspect of this process was the time commitment these women made. The pieces can be read quickly yet the writing process was anything but.

What I Learned

A question that I am invariably asked is, "What did you learn?" While I didn't set out to gather hard data, the consultant in me did discover some repeated themes. These themes include:

Intuition Rules: Intuition and guts were prominent qualities that helped these women land in a meaningful place. They were not going by a formula or a benchmark, but were propelled by their own internal engine. This explains how Lisa Person Weinberger ("A No-Regret Decision") knew that she couldn't return to her position in the law firm, or Jeanette Kuvin Oren knew that she needed to leave the study of epidemiology to become an artist ("The Art of the Career Choice").

"Meaningful" Counts Big Time: Sometimes the search for meaning was about coming full circle (Gretchen Dock and the farm, or Fran Heller who grew up speaking Spanish and later returned to serving a Latino population in healthcare). Some focused on identifying how they could feel more fulfilled in their work (Judy Elkin and coaching, or Ronna Benjamin with her passion for writing). For another, it was the adoption of her Chinese daughter that brought meaning to an otherwise very busy writer's life (Melissa Ludtke, "Cushioning My Landing"). The parachutes of these women were many colors and "meaning" was one of them.

Inch-by-Inch versus the Grand Plan: In many instances, these women did not conceive of some great plan that they could execute to achieve fulfillment. The style was more about figuring it out as they went along, making adjustments, and being open to what they learned along the way. In "Finding My Voice," Ellen Arad discovers the many ways she can parlay her love of music and singing into meaningful work. As Alyson Ferranti writes, it is really "A Series of Tweaks."

Duty Calls: Some were focused on the practical considerations of their lives as in managing children and travel (Kim Lorusso, "Falling off the Ladder"). For Deborah Mead (in "An Unhurried Life), she was able to tend to her ill father while following her passion for writing. Natalie Goldfein ("Channeling My Energy and Dreaming Big") postponed developing a new business to care for her mother during her last year of life. Many subscribed to the theory, expressed by one who chooses to remain anonymous, "You can have it all—just not all at once."

The Roaring Eighties: If we are lucky, we can be productive far longer than I had originally envisioned. The most inspiring moments came in working with the oldest group of women (seventy or eighty-plus) who are engaged and contributing in significant ways. Whether it is a retired math teacher doing civic duties (Jane Jamison, "The Corner of My Blackboard"), or some septuagenarians trying to instill the power of diversity in the workforce (Lee Gardenswartz, "Un Unpredictable Path" and Anita Rowe "Once a Teacher"), I felt slovenly in their company. I have since adjusted my own expectations. I want to be one of them.

So In a Nutshell …

At My Pace. features women's stories that show us that "life happens"—losses, setbacks, serendipity, and experiences all shape us. The grand plans for our lives that we might covet (*if* we covet) will probably change. The women in these essays met their world with their arms wide open. As Donna Surges Tatum's piece says, "Take a few left turns." Where these women take those turns, with whom, at what speed and conviction is what helps define them. Our travels might take us off-road and for a lot longer than we think, but with a strong stomach, we just might enjoy the experience.

You The Reader

In the spirit of "paying it forward," it would be a contribution by the readers to go online (www.atmypacebook.com) and provide feedback and maybe even something about your story. Did you have an ah-ha moment? Did you take a u-turn? Stare over a scary cliff? Take a fall and get up? Ride the autobahn at thrilling speed? Please share. We draw strength from the collective body of experience. My hope is that *At My Pace* is only a beginning.

A Disclaimer

Two degrees of separation—that is the relationship between me and the contributors of *At My Pace*. Because it is friends, and friends of friends, the group does not represent a cross-section of America, and many voices are left out. In the course of sharing this project with others, I was frequently asked the question, "What about those for whom 'at my pace' is not an option, or more difficult? There are single mothers, minimum-wage workers, those who do not have the opportunities for risky career or childcare decisions." This is not that book. This is a snapshot of a small sample of women and the choices they've made. It is my hope that *At My Pace* develops a readership, and that I have the opportunity to do a more inclusive sequel with more racial and economic diversity among the contributors.

Acknowledgements

There are many people to thank in the making of this book. First come the contributors, who are busy engaged in their life pursuits and yet were willing to take time and participate. Not only did I feel that the process gave me the gift of an excellent piece, but even better, I had the opportunity to get to know and learn from some inspiring women.

There was also a team of invisible hands that provided support, energy and ample skill. Were it not for them, this might have remained a "dream" project that never actually saw the light of day. First and foremost, I appreciate the many, many ways that my husband Steve supported this effort. His help came in all shapes and sizes—from proofreading, to brainstorming, to cheerleading, to helping me administer the process. To my sister Lee Gardenswartz and my friend Deborah Mead, thank you for consistently being an extra pair of eyes. Your insights were spot on and your support invaluable. To Ronna Benjamin, thank you for all your essential and pragmatic advice on publishing. Your guidance and resources provided critical short cuts to my steep learning curve. To my family (special shout out to my son and copy editor/proofreader Ari) and friends who won't be named because the list is too long, "thanks" feels too small for all the encouragement you have given me. So I will work off my debt by paying it forward, one person and one day at a time.

I. Women in Their 30s and 40s

Falling Off the Corporate Ladder

Kimberly Lorusso

With two demanding careers, two young kids, and erratic travel schedules, my husband and I were used to the inevitable question, "How *do* you guys do it?" From the outside, our lifestyle of juggling work, family, and social commitments looked like it was working out fine. On the inside, I was unraveling, and so was my husband.

One particular evening stands out as the first time I really felt the threads slip. The situation? Daycare pickup is at 6:00 p.m. It is now 5:45 p.m. My old college friend is sitting across from me on a disabled subway car (which was unfortunately becoming the norm–commuting into a city is everything but predictable). I have no cell phone service to call daycare, my husband is out of town, and I have no ETA on when we will be en route again. I feel trapped, helpless, and guilty. Would I, once again, be the last parent to pick up their children? Would my two kids be the only ones preventing daycare from locking up? Knowing me far too well, the look on my friend's face—a mix of empathy and concern—says it all. He knows I am on the verge of burnout.

Most weeknights after daycare pickup involve a hurried dinner around seven-thirty, followed by a rushed bedtime ritual so that I can get back to work. My days and nights are passing in a perpetual cycle of commuting and working.

I feel more undone when I take a look at my son's kindergarten schedule for the fall. It turns out that the "schedule" differs daily, and there is no school on Mondays. This is a working parent's nightmare and I break out into a sweat … again.

Something has to give.

After my husband and I finally find a quiet moment to talk about our challenging schedules, three things become clear: First, I need to accept that in our current scenario I can't make everything work to the standard I'd like. I know I am fortunate to have the set of problems caused by the too-full plate of being a parent, wife, and working professional. Believe me, I wouldn't trade my "problems" for someone else's, yet somehow I am not enjoying my bounty. Everything feels like a burden, and on particularly bad days, a Rubik's Cube that I can't solve.

Second, I realize that I need to reframe things. As an MBA, I've probably been subliminally programmed to climb the corporate ladder. After working so hard to establish my career, and leaning in for the last five years (and two kids' worth of motherhood), the personal and familial sacrifices are starting to mount. Now I need to consider stepping off the ladder, at least for a while.

Third, and perhaps most important, I need to be easier on myself. Even though I am performing well at work, my kids are off to a very good start, and I have a supportive husband, I still feel guilty and exhausted. I must shirk the feeling that I am failing at everything. I will no longer populate each sentence with an "I'm sorry."

Determined to find a way to make my situation work, I explore various daycare options and flexible work schedules. I start reading every article I can get my hands on about how to achieve work-life balance. Maybe there is some hidden gem that will unlock the mystery. Mentors, friends, and colleagues weigh in with lots of advice, only a smattering of which is useful to my specific situation. I decide that the term "work-life balance" is flawed and substitute "work-life integration" as a better objective.

I begin by tackling the flexible work arrangement, falsely confident that I will be successful because my employer is ranked as a top place for working mothers. After our conversations reveal that they will not accommodate me, I am devastated. After all, I love my career and want to keep it.

Left with no choice, I fall off the corporate ladder.

Now I am in unknown territory. My career defined so much of who I was, and the road ahead seems blurry and ill defined. Immediately, I start networking, and with the help of a few individuals with whom I will be eternally grateful, I find a few consulting projects. I settle on a new plan for now: Self-employment is my only real option for work-life integration. At least I can negotiate my schedule with my new boss.

While I am only two years into my career reinvention, and things are not perfect, my work-life integration plan is a huge improvement over the corporate ladder. Dinners and bedtime are much more in control with only my son's baseball game or daughter's ballet schedule wreaking occasional havoc. And we are not eating Costco roasted chicken nearly so often since I have some time for meal preparation. Sometimes I still miss key activities for my kids, but the overall blend is better and I am not ridden with guilt.

The process has taught me some important lessons. I know that I have limited capacity, that I too am a finite resource. I am more realistic about what is possible in a given day, week, or month, both personally and professionally. It is ok to say "no"—whether it's to a client, or in response to a request to chaperone a field trip. In my brave remade world, I am not as hard on myself.

What matters to me has changed. Trending down is money and prestige. Trending up is flexibility and rewarding work. In short, I have reframed my personal definition of success. The big fall off the corporate ladder is not about the bruises, but the blessings.

Taming the Unicorn

Christia Crocker

Sitting in a car outside a shopping center on a humid summer day with my cell phone in hand, my heart was in my throat, waiting for the call. My kids and I were at the end of a wonderful weeklong visit with my parents in the Midwest. The visit flooded me with memories where, as a child, I sang, danced, and performed in backyard swing-set extravaganzas and after-dinner talent shows. But now, my mind was consumed with what lay ahead for the kids and me back in Los Angeles. I was in a precarious financial struggle, and this call was for a job I needed more than any other in my life.

For the past two years, despite being an experienced entertainment attorney, I had been struggling to pay my bills after the collapse of my biggest client and the mixed results of others. My clients were important to me at many levels beyond financial wellbeing. They symbolized the boldness, creativity and freedom that I admire. My biggest client, a special effects company, was an anchor that had given me the stability and confidence to start a new life after the end of a near-decade of marriage. It was a scary time where, one-by-one, each leg of my life's table had been cut out from under me: First my marriage, then my job, then my hard-earned savings.

Beyond the shattered table, I was terrified that I would forever be stuck "on the outside" of traditional employment, and caught in the uncertain payment patterns of a solo practice. At one point in my career, I held a General Counsel position, so I knew the benefits of working for a company. I wanted to get back in-house and had been looking on and off for years. The feedback was always the same: they preferred applicants from large firms who were known commodities. It was hard to know what to make of my nine hard-won years running a solo practice. I would console myself that after all, it was a recession. There was a glut of legal talent on the market. But the personal repercussions were huge. My confidence was shot. I cursed myself for leaving the work-force after starting a family. I felt stuck, ashamed, and irrelevant.

By nature or nurture I have always been a hard worker, holding down multiple jobs until I became a mother. My dad's favorite motto, "Work is a privilege," rang true to me. I had my first job at thirteen, was financially independent and debt-free by twenty-one. After graduating college, I used my double major in theatre and modern dance choreography to tell stories through video projects and screenplays. Work evolved as I grew from jobs in production to business development. Graduate school beckoned as I looked at the credentials of the studio execs around me, and so I went to law school. Upon graduation I was hired by Creative Arts Agency (CAA), where I sacrificed good pay for the pleasure of being in the entertainment industry.

Walking through the hallowed halls of CAA in the early morning before my boss arrived, I felt as if I belonged. I was certain I would never need to start from scratch ever again. I believed I had the finesse and winning combination of lawyer and creative mind to be an asset to any production.

Then I had my first child, and the path to becoming an agency executive became fraught with issues.

I was unprepared for the life-change of nursing and caring for a newborn around-the-clock. With no family nearby, I couldn't make sense of passing my daughter off to a nanny who was unrelated, and would probably cost me more than the tender wages I received. I made the decision to resign to the delight of everyone around me. My former husband, my family and friends all thought that this was a natural decision, justified by my ex's respectable salary. The downside was not apparent at the time. My discomfort at being completely financial dependent for the first time since adolescence and the gnawing angst of an abandoned career left me vowing to start a legal practice once I had motherhood down.

I underestimated what it would take to get a handle on motherhood. I likened it to the ease of finding and taming a unicorn. Balance and a consistent flow to daily life were hard to achieve. Building relationships was elusive. Since theatre had been much of my life, I tried to imagine that every day was just another improvisation—unpredictable and living in the moment. I would need to forget metrics. No ranking or grade or diploma awaited me.

Over the next several years, I built a practice while I worked on integrating parenting with work. This led to many unusual moments, like the time I took my son, who was less than one and not yet walking, to a pitch meeting with five network executives! The babysitter was not available and so I broke protocol in order to not lose the deal. There we were—everyone was suited up, attentively reading the non-disclosure agreements I had drafted, while I held my squirming son on my hip.

Moments like these were stark reminders of my lack of available family support, and the creative solutions we come upon. Most of these solutions are just old-fashioned hard work done at odd hours so that we can maximize our time with kids during the day. Despite all odds, I had managed to grow into an attorney that I was proud of, pitching and selling footage, helping launch new corporate entities, winning in court or getting favorable settlements against legal goliaths. I felt I was a valued resource at my clients' side, and I was not about to be told that these years of sacrifices did not count.

And then the phone rang—I didn't get the job.

Like life itself, the conversation was not as straightforward as I would have hoped. Still I took stock in how far I had come and for how long. After all the let-downs, I realized that I would persevere. My path was authentic, defined in my early days of motherhood, and has been evolving ever since. There may not be a grand re-entry for me into a hallowed company. I am learning to be OK with that. My kids have shown me that growth often happens in small imperceptible ways, rather than the epic moments we often fantasize about. So I will follow their lead, stay in the moment, continue to grow, and who knows ... maybe find and tame that unicorn, yet!

Editor's note: As this book goes to print, a happy phone call finally came.

The Trail to
Mindful Nourishment

Allyson Straka

If we are the sum of our experiences, then my sum must be big. From an early age I was a closet geek, afraid to tell people that I loved computers. I wanted to be cool and being a girl who liked computers was anything but cool. So instead, as the only girl in my computer class, I told everyone I was a teacher's assistant. That seemed to provide adequate cover.

Today I am a thirty-six year old mom with two kids and a husband that I'll call "Mr. Google" because he works in advertising at Google. Between being a "Teacher's Assistant" and a mom who started her own business, there have been many stops along the way. Lets start with a low point: I used to be a drug addict and dropped out of school for a year to get myself clean, for I believe that we must place ourselves firmly behind the wheel of own our lives. After treatment, I went to Indiana University where I completed my undergraduate degree. While there, I worked part time at a real estate company, mostly so that I could stay busy and not think about drugs. While there I also realized the splendor of working in a small company where you could see the difference you made, and it didn't take years.

After college came the technology carousel I rode. I began by working for several start-up companies of which one was eventually acquired by Microsoft. At the time, I was very excited. A job at Microsoft was a geek's dream, come true. Shortly thereafter I realized how much I actually hated the job. The culture felt male-dominated. Things took so long to get done, especially when compared to my small company experience. Most importantly, I realized that trying to be the next person to get promoted at Microsoft with "X" number of people working under me was old-school thinking and wouldn't make me happy. This ah-ha moment seems obvious in retrospect but was a major discovery at the time.

I left Microsoft and returned to the Midwest and once again experienced the pleasures of small company living. The only issue was that not long after settling in, I had my first child. While I was able to wrangle a return back after an extended maternity leave, I heard some internal voice wooing me to be a stay-at-home mom.

With my husband's support, I left a very good company and became a full-time Mom. While I knew I was lucky for the opportunity to stay home, I soon realized that I did not love my new status. I was used to validation and not feeling it. I was used to stimulation and getting out, and wearing nice clothes (not fancy, just nice), and this was a whole new rhythm where days kind of ran into each other. I decided I needed a "passion project" for stimulation, to open up my world.

To understand my next move, I need to digress and explain that I have always been very aware of what goes into my body. I am not completely sure its origins, but twice in my life, I ventured on the Appalachian Trail for substantial periods—ninety-three and then seventy-two days. There is nothing like hiking the trail to make you aware of what you are consuming. My interest in nutrition became the source of my passion project. I enrolled at the Institute of Integrative Nutrition (IIN), thinking it would add to my knowledge and help me do better a job of managing my family's nutrition.

Here is where the unexpected serendipity occurs. I morphed my passion project into a business with two simple goals: To get outside of the house on a limited basis (two days per week on average), and to cover my expenses. Shortly after attending IIN, I became product-focused and created some workshops, a whole foods cleanse, and accompanying personal coaching. I wanted to help people take ownership of their health—put them in the driver's seat, so to speak—much like I had done when my life veered off course.

Mindful Nourishment, the name of my company, has now been running for over two years and combines my love of business with nutrition. I am both proud and shocked that during that time, we have serviced nearly five-hundred clients. I have had to hire two health coaches to make this happen. I also needed to wear a sales hat, use simple technology like blogs to build awareness, and make sure I hire the right people to support this venture.

We have been very busy and anticipate continued growth. Corporations continue to approach me about running programs for their employees. A hospital system, interested in integrating our program with patient care, just recently signed an agreement. The health coaches will work alongside physicians in a holistic effort to manage patients. This will mean more hiring. All the while, I am sticking with my reduced schedule so that I can spend primetime with my children.

It is hard to say what is next. My passion project has turned into a legitimate business. Mr. Google (aka, my husband) would like to know my end game. I wish I could say, but right now I love that I get to field a good team, help people groove healthier habits, and think big in terms of who we collaborate with to extend our reach. Never far from my mind though is finishing the last stretch of the Appalachian Trail—from Connecticut to Maine— that I have yet to complete. There will be a difference in how I do it, which says a lot about my personal journey. The previous trips were very solo experiences where I needed to prove to myself that I was strong and whole. Completion of the trail will hopefully involve my family. I have learned how much I need them to be the independent and healthy person that I strive to be.

Celebrating My Choices

Hillary Gardenswartz

There I was, standing at Columbus Circle on that first Sunday in November. Runners were reaching their twenty-sixth mile with 0.2 miles to go before crossing the finish line. I had been living in New York City for several years and still it never ceased to amaze me, each first Sunday in November—how awesome those runners looked. Droves of people from all over funneling into that final turn into Central Park could do this crazy thing called a marathon. They looked so ordinary doing this extraordinary thing, that after a few years of spectating, it finally occurred to me, "Huh, if these people can do this, people of all shapes and sizes, maybe I can, too."

There was just one problem: I hated running.

I have always been a person who, when set on doing something, likes to get that thing done. I call it "trait determination." Some call it "stubbornness." I have never been the type to shrink from hard work or challenges, though losing, being wrong, or stumbling along the way is really difficult for me. My aunt occasionally likes to remind me of the time I was five years old and resorted to cheating in a round of Memory because I couldn't bear losing. I'd like to think I've matured since my card-cheating days of yore, but my desire to come out on top still exists (though hopefully in healthier ways!)

Determined to set my own course throughout my life, I also assumed I'd follow a somewhat predictable path: degree, job, marriage, children, community involvement, etc. The degree and job seemed like no-brainers. I spent my twenties getting my degrees and entering the working world. My choices about education and work seemed pretty on-track, which in some ways made them feel like not real "choices" at all. I could check off my imaginary boxes next to "education" and "profession." But what about the husband and kids? Shouldn't those "choices" also be falling into place?

It's not like I was actively choosing or not choosing to find a life partner and move into the next stage that most of my friends had already entered. It just hadn't happened for me. The predicted path wasn't working out in reality like it had always played out in my head. I had earned a degree in Talmud and was teaching these ancient texts through my own modern lens, yet somehow that seemed less provocative than being an unmarried woman in her early thirties. Women have made unbelievable progress in the fight for social equality in the past fifty years; I stand on their shoulders as a proud feminist. Yet even in the twenty-first century, when marriage and children are not part of a woman's narrative, questions about worth and fulfillment and meaning seem to creep into the ether in an invasive and haunting way.

Growing up in a traditional Jewish home, family, community, education, and ritual played central roles. And while my parents encouraged all their children to pursue their education and passions with egalitarian vigor, nevertheless traditional gender roles and family structure remained the dominant paradigm through which I experienced life. Both American society and Jewish tradition prize the traditional family structure. The milestones that help define that path—marriage, births, bar/bat mitzvah, anniversaries—provide built-in moments of support and celebration. But what about people who do not make those choices or fall into that structure? What about people who are single? Or childless? Who celebrates *those* choices? Who celebrates *me?*

Deciding to run the marathon felt like the first true choice I had made on my own behalf as an adult. It wasn't a choice that was part of an assumed path. It wasn't a choice that anyone expected from me. It was a choice for me, by me. And once I decided that I was going to run the marathon, that was it—no turning back. Even if I hated running before, I would figure it out. There was a greater goal in mind.

One of my close friends had just completed the race in 2011, and at her post-race celebration I looked at another friend and we said, "Let's do it." Two nights later we were out on the streets of New York for our very first training run. I had no clue what I was getting myself into. But over the next year my training partner and I ran together, joined a charity team that provided coaching and support, and slogged our way through mile after mile until we were ready to go.

After one full year of training, hundreds of miles, countless sore muscles and ice baths under our belts, Superstorm Sandy hit.

Marathon cancelled. Devastation. Done.

I was bereft and depressed. The thought of training a whole other year felt unbelievable. But I also knew, for me, there was no other choice. I was running this damn marathon come hell or high water, literally. And through the seemingly endless miles, muscle aches, and enough Beyoncé tunes until I was singing in my sleep, I made it through another year of training. In that year I was able to learn more about myself as a runner, and more importantly, more about myself as a person. It was when the choice I had made to run the marathon was taken away from me, that I realized the strength and independence implicit in my decision.

This realization became most clear in the context of my family. For a variety of reasons, my immediate family was not going to be physically present to cheer me on at the race in 2012. At the time I shrugged it off. When the marathon was cancelled and I started to unpack my emotional response of the entire experience, I realized how important it was for me to have them there. Their presence would not only provide strength and encouragement along the route, but it would also be an affirmation of me and my choices, a celebration that even if my life doesn't follow the predictable path, I'm worthy of being celebrated for the choices I *do* make, in all their iterations. We might have to try a bit harder to find ways of recognizing moments outside conventional norms—they do exist, and deserve our celebration as well.

As I ran through the five boroughs for the first time in 2013, my family was there every step of the way (some of them literally running parts of the race with me!) I crossed the finish line of my very first marathon, the very first real choice I ever made. I cried in celebration. And so did my family.

Finding My Own Brand

Laurel Mintz

You can call it marching to the beat of my own drum, but I like to think of it as creating a life at my own pace.

I've always been that way. Perhaps my upbringing had a great deal to do with it. My dad was a hippy in the '60s and lived in Laurel Canyon. Being born and raised in LA, I was named after the infamous canyon (hence Laurel). To this day, I live and work less than ten minutes from where I grew up, but not without taking a journey to bring me back to where it all started.

To be honest, I never thought I would be a business owner; I always thought I would be a lawyer. When I applied to law school, my essay was on how I negotiated a later bedtime with my parents every night. I was that good.

Law school itself did not provide the fit I had imagined as I never found an area of law that I was passionate about. In 2006, I graduated with a JD and an MBA with an emphasis in marketing from Rutgers University. I migrated back to Los Angeles to bask in California's sunshine and escape the harsh winters of the East Coast. Having worked in a marketing capacity for top restaurateurs and launching several national brands, I aspired to the six-figure job in a downtown tower corner office. Fortunately for me, life had a different agenda.

Soon after returning to Los Angeles, I found out that my father had stage-four bladder cancer. To ensure my family could survive financially, I put my career trajectory on hold and stepped in to run my family business for two years. Our retail business had a staff of more than forty people; I was the youngest and in charge. Suddenly I was applying newly minted skills to the tasks of merchandising, marketing, ad buying, sales, training, and other areas that a small business needs to thrive. It was the fastest education in business ownership I could ever have asked for. I remember sitting in the office thinking that any day now, they would figure out that I had no idea what I was doing. Somehow, that never happened. Most fortunate was that my dad survived the disease and was able to step back into the business, freeing me up to get back onto my previous path.

As I started interviewing and getting offers, I felt a strong visceral response at the thought of working for someone else. The idea that I would spend fifty-plus hours a week making someone else rich in an area that I was lukewarm about was not my idea of a purposeful life.

I began networking and using my relationships with local retailers to determine how I could put both of my degrees to work. Thus began my start in consulting, and developing marketing plans, again all new to me. I discovered that consulting could enable me to build a solid career. I started and grew two different consulting firms and learned what kind of clients and projects best suited me.

After working with a multitude of businesses and of course through trial and error, I found my true passion, and in 2010, Elevate My Brand was born. Like most startups, we started in my tiny rent-controlled apartment and expanded rapidly from there. Our company offers strategy development and execution for brands helping them to be more visible and more profitable through branding, digital content, live events, etc., and it has been both an exciting and terrifying ride. We get to work with remarkable businesses, and proceed up the learning curve of how to operate a business and make something from nothing.

It's not easy, and in fact there are many days when I think a smart person would have taken a safer path, a previous offer. My mood changes though when I see the appreciation from clients—flowers, a card, or a grateful hug. It reminds me that we are helping to make an impact.

As if all of the other signs were not enough, the current Elevate My Brand offices are in a personally iconic building that I used to pass every day on my way to high school. It has remained a poignant reminder of my journey and my hard-won accomplishments.

I am very lucky to say that during this self-discovery process, just as I started my agency, I met the man of my dreams. Mike is also an entrepreneur, which makes it easier to understand each other, and the long fourteen-plus hour days that are sometimes necessary. For us, wading through the pile of takeout menus is a common occurrence. Together we have made the conscious decision that we don't want children—not because we don't love them or think we would be good parents. We just aren't ready to give up the lifestyle that we have created for ourselves.

My incredible journey back to where it all started has also taught me a few lessons along the way. Nothing has been more important than the people. With the right complement of talent, chemistry, and trust, we can do some amazing things. That is the biggest lesson I learned: Creating a successful life and business and finding pace that works for you is only possible by surrounding yourself with truly excellent people that share you values. I am forever thankful for the "invisible hands" behind Elevate My Brand.

The Quest for Daily Balance

Megan Laufman

My whole life, I've always strived to find balance. As a teenager in high school, I recall having regular debates with my parents who encouraged me to apply myself more to my AP classes and SAT prep and to focus more while doing homework rather than talking on the phone. My response to them always came with a huffy tone: "Mom, Dad—I know what I need to do to get into a good college and trust me, I will do that, but my social life is equally important and I am not going to give up having fun in the process." That was 1994.

Fast forward to the year 2000, when I graduated from the University of California at Santa Barbara; continuing in my life's mantra, I definitely had my fair share of fun (maybe too much of it), while I also managed to complete a year abroad in London, where I traveled and studied equal parts—proof that "balance" is possible.

After graduation, I started my career in advertising. The ad agency culture is youthful and cutting edge and I had a blast as a

Media Buyer. Days consisted of work blended in with long, fancy lunches and ended with late nights out, leaving the bar at last call. While I loved every minute, I noticed that I had lost sight of the balance. The scale was all tilted to the fun side, and I knew I needed a change. It was at about that time that I started dating my soon-to-be husband. With the fearlessness and invincibility of a twenty-something, I decided to make a major career change.

With my parents and boyfriend's support, I began a career in Commercial Real Estate. This was a hard, pure commission job, yet it was incredibly rewarding. I built my business from scratch and made more than I could have dreamed of as a twenty-five-year-old. Yet I was frustrated by the constraints of working in a male-dominated world. For the majority of my tenure, I was the only female agent in an office of fifty and in a loosely defined environment with no boundaries, you can imagine the situations I was privy to ... just think *locker room*. I looked around and witnessed families falling apart, substance abuse, and loose ethics. It wasn't a healthy environment, and I realized it didn't resonate with me, as my husband and I were beginning to think about starting a family. This was not the type of job I wanted my children to see their mother doing, and so I decided to leave with no job lined up.

A few months later, I started the next chapter—a career in Executive Search—and seven years later, here I am. During this time, I had two children and truly feel that someone upstairs was looking out for me in granting me this job, with this company, at this time. I enjoy what I do but am mostly appreciative that this job allows me the balance I seek. My company supports tele-commuting, and I work mostly from home. Most importantly, I have a boss who is incredibly supportive. He encourages me to take ten a.m. yoga classes in the middle of my workday and doesn't question when I have a school event for my kids or a doctor's appointment to run to. Often times, he and I are catching up and strategizing mid-day, and I let him know I have to run to pick up my son at one o'clock from school. I pinch myself. How did I get so lucky to have a mentally stimulating, financially rewarding career while also being able to be a hands-on mom?

Of course, it is not always ideal and as perfect as I paint it out to be. After having my second child, I had a strong desire to stay home full-time with my kids. I couldn't imagine not. My anxiety about returning to work escalated when two months after my daughter was born, my son became seriously ill. After specialist visits and testing, he was diagnosed with Chronic Benign Neutropenia. We were in shock and were consumed with fear while they spent three months reaching the diagnosis. The good news was that he would eventually outgrow this condition, but the process required our little three-year-old son to undergo a bone marrow aspiration and many weekly blood draws. As I pondered our situation, it all felt so surreal, and it was at that point in my life that my priorities became clearer than ever.

I knew in a different kind of way that my family and our combined health and happiness were more important than anything else in the world. Work didn't matter, nor did trivial matters that used to suck me in. As time passed and life normalized, I eventually came back to center and life resumed. But I had been willing to put my career on hold, indefinitely, without a second thought. I would be lying if I didn't say that there are times that I struggle with my career path and feel internal pressure to take the leap. I have conversations in my head with my internal board of directors, each one weighing in on the pros and cons. Thus far, no matter how many times I run through the scenarios, I have consistently come to the conclusion that there is no need to rock the boat. I am ever so grateful for the ability to be both a hands-on mom while balancing a full time career. And yes, I may be missing out a bit in compensation and a more glorified title, but at least I am staying true to the balance that I have valued since my earliest days.

A Series of Tweaks

Alyson Ferranti

$\mathbf{M}$y journey can be defined as a series of tweaks. Getting it right out of the gate would not have been possible. New realities continued to emerge—children, challenging projects and heavy workloads, and my own growing self-confidence. And so, at the appropriate time, and after a series of incremental adjustments, I made a major (and somewhat frightening) adjustment to become my own boss, emboldened by a mix of naïveté and optimism. I can say *now* that I am glad I did.

My story begins with my passion for market research. My interest is probably traceable to my early childhood years when the mother of an elementary school friend asked me to participate in some local focus groups. The topics ranged from peanut butter to sneakers to anything a child might have influence on as their parents waded through the onslaught of child-focused marketing efforts. I loved the experience, though I couldn't have articulated back then that this would become my livelihood.

Though I'd held some other research positions coming out of college, at twenty-seven I landed the job that would ultimately define my path into strategic market research. A boutique-consulting firm hired me, and I quickly conquered the learning curve, engaging in complex projects, all in a virtual environment. I loved the work and didn't mind the long hours. My very first project necessitated I work on a Friday night while my fiancé went out with friends. There I was, by myself, burning the midnight oil, fortified by a bowl of ice cream and a glass of wine. Little did I know that those hours were a harbinger of things to come.

The market researcher in me wants to share my demographics: I am in my thirties, married with two children, and living in an upper middle class area in the Northeast. While we are blessed to have two children, they didn't come easy. We endured a period of infertility that made work a welcome respite from our feelings of hopelessness. Then after two rounds of in-vitro fertilization, our son was born. And because life is never without its twists, just one month before the baby's arrival, my husband was laid-off. The stress of managing with only one income was palpable, but so was the joy of spending three months together at home with our newborn. Check one off for blessings in disguise.

When maternity leave came to an end, our son's grandmothers were eager to take on babysitting duties. I was raring to go, determined to prove that I could "do it all." And for a while, I think that I actually did. With an incredibly supportive family, daycare and a husband who shared equal duty, we were making it work. But suddenly my hours started to become very odd. Some days I stopped work at a reasonable hour but then spent late nights and early mornings finishing what my "early" departure had left.

Because I worked from home, the boundaries became more than blurry—they downright failed to exist. Life became unbalanced, but I was still patting myself on the back that I was "doing it."

Then a very welcome surprise hit. When my son was still an infant himself, I saw something that had eluded us for years: a positive pregnancy test. We were ecstatic and in shock. The uncertainty of managing "two under two" was eclipsed by the joy of a miracle we didn't think possible.

After our daughter's birth, new realities emerged in terms of my work life. Of course there was extreme fatigue, but there was also the loss of my home office space – my quiet place was now a nursery. Amidst Boppy pillows and Jumperoos, the dining room table became where I spent my nine-to-five (and then some). I was still aiming to "do it all," convinced that appropriate focus, multitasking skills, and a strong support system would win the day. Plus, we instituted a new tweak: My husband would take paternity leave after my maternity leave was over. It enabled me to have a smoother transition back to work and became an opportunity for my husband to be at the helm, something most men never have.

When paternity leave came to an end, the Grammie Brigade was once again enlisted, along with daycare. Each day there were drop-offs and pick-ups at different locations, and a negotiation with my husband as to who did what. My work was more demanding than ever, and I continued to burn the candle at both ends.

While I knew this would not be sustainable in the long-term, the over-achiever in me was hoping that I could somehow achieve success at the full-time-working-mom-thing. Ultimately something had to give, and the tipping point came after a discussion with a superior. Being a new mom herself, I anticipated empathy when we broached the topic of *the challenges of balancing work and family.* But when she suggested that I might want to re-evaluate my child-care I knew what that really meant "more coverage." As I listened, I quietly did the math in my head: drop-off at 7:30 a.m. and pick-up at 5:30 p.m. Let's see, that's ten hours of daycare—surely this was ample time to have a full, productive workday, right?

Though I knew the time was coming, this conversation proved to be motivation to pursue a different kind of work life. I almost accepted a position with a company that was similar to my current situation, but when my plane got re-routed on my way to the final interview, I considered this a sign from above to veer differently.

That aborted plane trip was two years ago. I have since started my own market research practice, and while setting boundaries is still a challenge, the difference now is that I report to me. It might sound ideal, but challenges remain. Odd hours, no one to pass the buck to, two children who have always had a voice, but now have lots of words! Clients will change, the kids will have new interests, life will bring new twists, so I know there will be more tweaks. If I have learned anything it's that trying to plan for an ideal future is a strategy that just doesn't fit my life. Rather, I've learned to adjust to the now.

A No-Regret Decision

Lisa Pierson Weinberger

At 11:38 p.m. on October 14, 2009, my life changed forever. As I lay in the operating room undergoing an emergency C-section, I heard my baby cry out for the first time. Though I knew motherhood would have a profound impact on my life, I did not know that it would trigger a personal metamorphosis.

My story begins with some context. When I was growing up, my parents went through a period of financial upheaval that had a traumatic affect on me. It left a palpable angst when as a junior in college, I was trying to figure out what to do professionally. I wanted to guard against financial vulnerability. So, with pragmatism and employability top of mind, I decided to head straight to law school. I tabled the question of personal passions and went to UCLA Law School, where I started a new life.

Luck struck right at the beginning when, during orientation, I spotted a handsome guy across the courtyard. Dan would eventually become my husband. That was the good news of law school, along with a good job when I graduated. I didn't enjoy law school itself—the constant stress and pressure—but it yielded the financial security I so badly sought.

My early days in "the firm" were quite good. I worked with the partners and received accolades. I could pay off my school loans and build a cushion. I was on track for "success"—at the right place, doing the right thing, at the right time. I didn't mind the long hours that extended into weekends. My husband worked long hours, too, and it all worked until I held my child for the first time.

Many women honestly admit that they did not connect with their babies immediately. Not so for me. I was sure that Ethan was the cutest, sweetest, and smartest child ever born. All that joy was followed by six very hard months, where I took time off to learn how to be a mom. Together Ethan and I were figuring it out.

As I neared the end of my maternity leave, I had what can only be described as a personal crisis. I had always prided myself on my professional achievements and declared how important it was for children to see their mothers work and for women to have lives outside of their families. Yet, the thought of leaving Ethan in someone else's care and going back to work had me in a panic. I frantically crunched numbers to see if we could survive financially without my income; we couldn't. I took Ethan to daycare and hoped he would stop crying when I left. He didn't. This new predicament, and my reaction to it, was not what I expected.

My firm graciously honored my request to work part-time. I then interviewed fifteen nannies before finding Melissa, an angel sent from heaven to save me and anchor Ethan. With my breast pump in tow, crying in the car, I went back to work.

After a while, I got used to the new routine. I pumped at work though I despised it. I was able to leave Ethan with Melissa, who we both grew to love. I reawakened in me the satisfaction of being a professional and using my education to help people. The problem was that now I did mind working nights and weekends; I did mind the politics of the law firm; I did mind that my schedule was at the mercy of clients and partners. And I didn't always like whom I represented or the side of the issue I was on. In short, I realized that somewhere out there would be a professional opportunity worth my sacrificing time with Ethan, but the law firm was not it. I needed to make a change.

This time around as I considered my options, added other factors into the equation. What could I successfully balance? How could I contribute to my community? I knew that I wanted to be with Ethan, whenever I wanted, no permission required. I realized that I needed to be my own boss.

In February 2011, Mom Esq. was born, dedicated to the employment needs of parents. I help women understand and maximize their maternity leave benefits, enforce reinstatement and lactation rights following leaves of absence, negotiate for part-time and flexible schedules, and counsel families on how to properly employ their domestic help. I work from my office, my home, and even my car en route to an "Ethan Pick-Up." I often work in sweats, and I regularly work late into the night because I've spent traditional working hours being a mom. My clients range from those who live paycheck to paycheck to the very wealthy. I have found that we are the same in the ways that matter most: We are doing our best to raise our children in an ever-complicated world. We wear so many hats, and not always comfortably.

A few weeks ago, a woman who used to sit on a Board of Directors with me in my pre-Ethan life called me for some professional help. Since we had last worked together, she had gotten married and had recently become a mother. When she went back to work she was still breastfeeding and her employer was requiring her to pump in a shower stall in the lobby of the building in which she worked. She was distraught. It's amazing how quickly employers can become accommodating when they receive a letter from a lawyer, and I was thrilled to be able to help my former colleague enforce her rights at work. This was a small matter, and one that I would not have been able to take on had I still been working at my former firm. Being able to help other mothers, and do work that feels honorable, has added much to my life.

There is a P.S. to my story. Through a medical miracle, several surgeries and IVF treatments, I am now the proud mother of Noa, my two-year-old daughter. Her birth brought new appreciation of life's blessings and reinforced the choices I've made. On hard days, I remind myself that the stress and mess doesn't matter because in the words of my wise husband, I've made a "no regret" decision: I will never look back at the time spent with my children and regret any moment of it.

II. Women in Their 50s and 60s

Wild Cat Mountain Revisited

Susana Fonticoba

One lovely fall day, when my husband and I were in our mid-twenties, fun-loving and carefree, we went to New Hampshire for the weekend. Admiring Wildcat Mountain, we rode the ski lift to the summit to take some photos. After a while, my husband looked down toward the base and exclaimed that we should skip the lift and walk back down. It would be a lovely hike and we'd make it down in about an hour. It sounded like fun; we headed down. After walking for an hour and a half and being nowhere near the mid-point, we realized that this must be why we were the only idiots hiking down, while everyone else zipped past us on the ski lift. Two hours in, and it was difficult to tell how much closer we had gotten. I was miserable and frustrated, and plopped myself down on a large rock to pout and complain.

Then came the pep talk. Fully realizing how he had misjudged the distance, and checking his watch to quickly calculate how soon it would get dark, my husband scolded me for even thinking of taking a break. "What are you hoping for, someone to come along and give you a ride down? There's no way down but to continue walking, no matter how tired you are. By stopping you're going nowhere! Now get up!" Of course he was right, and another hour and a half saw us safely reach the bottom, just a bit before sun down.

Thirty years later, I realize that I often reach silently for that speech.

My husband passed away at the age of forty-three. I was unprepared to be a forty-two-year-old widow, and single mother of two girls, aged ten and fourteen. How was I supposed to manage this? As a widow, I had been plopped back on that mountain, taking one step, one day at a time, with no hope of being rescued. I was still fortunate—I had my family, new widow friends and a steady job.

Just when I thought I could become comfortable in my new life, the mountain suddenly got taller—I was downsized from my corporate job. Now the way down seemed more treacherous, and once again, I had no opportunity for a "time-out."

Most of my new widow friends were much older than me, but we clung to each other for support nonetheless. One of them was apprehensive when using her computer and I came to her rescue several times. With no job and no spouse, I helped her learn her way around AOL to keep my sanity. One day she suggested that others like her were also struggling with their PCs; since no one was hiring, I could simply create my own job. It's madness, I thought. I had no experience being a business owner; but, then, I had been no hiker, either.

I spread the word and soon I was in business, coming to the rescue of many a senior lost in the world of Windows and AOL. While the money was a fraction of what I used to earn, my new job was helping me become a whole person again. Along the hike down of my own personal Wildcat Mountain, life changed in many ways. I became business savvy and gained a confidence I would never have foreseen. Joining a professional organization, I was soon on its leadership team, then became president, and all the while I developed my business.

Suddenly I wasn't in a hurry to climb down that mountain; I felt invigorated by exploring new walking trails. Life is not a series of challenges you need to hurry through. There are winding paths that may appear risky, but when you decide to explore, a whole new panorama opens up. Over the years I had to stand strong and survive major events without my husband: graduations, walking my daughter down the aisle, the girls moving out as adults.

In my business, I discovered more needs for my skills as a business software coach, and I left the AOL ladies to explore more services I could offer. Of course no hike is smooth and without incident , and for a while I felt as if I had climbed down a completely wrong lane. Progress stopped and indeed I found myself in a place further up the mountain with no clue how to find the road down. I sat on the rock one more time, pouting and complaining. I could hear my husband's voice giving me the pep talk again.

I had to admit my business was failing. There were three months of panic and confusion. What to do now? My widow friend who had inspired with the idea of the tutoring business passed away during this time. Did I ever really thank her enough for giving me a new future? And who was going to help me discover another path?

Luckily, one of the computer programs I had been using to market my business was Constant Contact, and I looked into their affiliate programs. I learned I could sell their product and also make money providing related services. I firmly shut the door on my old business, closing that lane and continuing the hike down my new path.

Sometimes I allow myself the luxury of thinking back to my ever-continuing personal development. Or as I call it, growing up. I started out as a shy wife of a man who was bigger than life. If the young woman in her twenties could meet this mid-fifties woman, she would be completely astonished. Somehow I had managed to climb down a mountain that was far higher and more confusing than Wildcat, and although my coach would not be by my side, he was always in my heart, reminding me to get down on my own, to keep walking, because no one was going to rescue me. It's a powerful lesson, one I hold onto every day.

Finding My Passion After 50

Ronna Benjamin

The year I graduated college, 1980, was not a good year for me. I was dumped by the guy I was in love with (he realized he was gay a year after dating me), I was in the throes of trying to deal with an eating disorder, and I had a "made up" major at my university, one that I was not totally confident in. It combined a lot of religious studies and philosophy classes—not particularly useful in the job market.

I ignored the recruiters who arrived on campus in early spring to interview the seniors for jobs. Banking? Unlikely. Accounting? Not a chance. PR? Not for me.

The fact that I had no idea what I wanted to do when I graduated college frightened and embarrassed me, but it freaked my parents out even more. It was not a time when parents encouraged their kids to take a year off to get their act together and "find" themselves, and it was not a time when kids simply moved home (god forbid!) after graduation.

That spring, my twenty-first year, with no job prospects, no passion to follow, and certainly no love of the law, I ended up, by default, applying to law school. It was actually my mother's idea (I think I might have said,"hmmm, that sounds good . . . ") I was stunned into silence when people asked me what area of the law I was interested in.

"Uh ... *none?*"

That did not seem an acceptable answer.

Law school turned out to be pretty good (other than the classes). I met an awesome guy, became engaged the night before graduation, and despite not having developed a passion either in or out of the law, I got a great job in the real estate department of a large Boston law firm.

I bought high heels and dark suits. My husband and I walked to our downtown law offices. He kissed me goodbye outside a high rise where I took the elevator up to the twenty-ninth floor. I had an office with a view and my own secretary. It felt good, and I tried like hell to get excited about fee titles, deeds, and wraparound mortgages.

But it didn't work.

Following the birth of our first child, an adorable little girl, I very consciously *leaned out.*

I couldn't stand the thought of leaving my baby to go to work that I didn't feel excited about. Soon after, I started working part time as the lawyer for a family real estate company that offered me flexible hours, and much later I worked part time out of my home.

Our family grew to three kids, a yellow lab, and a house in the suburbs. I carpooled the kids, went to their games, became President of the PTO, swept dog hair from the kitchen floor, and cooked fabulous family dinners from big yellow *Gourmet Cookbook*, which became my bible.

All the while, I continued my law practice. I took calls from clients complaining about the hole in the rug, or the flooded basement, or the word "hereinafter" in the agreement. I began to despise reading and negotiating contracts—the small print, the nastiness, the detail. I even began to resent my clients, who *always* seemed to call me when the minivan was full of kids.

I never loved "lawyering," but I began to hate it.

I realized what I really wanted was a Passion. How come everyone else seemed to have a Passion? How come I didn't? Where could I find mine? I ached to do work I loved.

I started trying a few things on, hoping to find my Passion. I tried to be passionate about growing orchards; they died. I tried to be passionate about stringing beads; I got bored. I tried to be passionate about my fabulous meringue cookies, but they ended up with dog hair in them. Nothing stuck.

And then, facing a completely empty nest, peri-menopause struck. I often found myself up between four and six in the morning with nothing to do.

One night, inspired by a Saturday evening dinner out with an unbelievably wealthy, supercilious, narcissistic jerk (nope, I'm not naming names), I sat down at my computer and wrote about the dinner. And I laughed as I wrote, and then I laughed some more. And that's how I got hooked.

I didn't think about the negatives: I had never taken a writing course. I hadn't written anything creative since high school. I had no idea how writing was going to make any money.

It really never occurred to me then that I had found my Passion. But when I found myself awake at four a.m., I smiled, got out of bed, and automatically sat down at my computer to write. And as I wrote, I continued to laugh.

I was introduced to betterafter50.com, an online magazine for women over fifty, the day after founder Felice Shapiro took it live. The timing was right. Felice was looking for submissions, and I was writing funny stories about life after fifty in the middle of the night.

Within eight months, Felice and I became not only great friends, but also business partners at betterafter50.com. Together, we have grown the business to over two million views a month and we just published our first book, *We Are Better After 50 Because…*

I have loved every minute.

I no longer seek my Passion; I have earned it. I am learning something new each day in this new chapter of my life—about social media, sales, marketing, writing—things that I could never have imagined myself doing in my first chapter. It is not always easy. I am often overwhelmed. I am often out of my comfort zone.

But it is a rare day that I am not laughing while working. Perhaps that is what having a Passion is all about.

Zigs And Zags
And Floor-Drops

Nancy Strehlow

I've made some changes in the direction and pace of my life that I used to consider pretty dramatic: from artist to litigator, from litigator to stay-at-home-mom, from full-time mom to part-time in-house lawyer. Those changes, however, were alterations in course, not changes in the road map that I consult to plot out my life. They were changes in the role I was choosing to play, rather than the collapse of the stage upon which I was standing. They were significant changes, but not of the same caliber, or even the same species, as the changes that occurred last spring, when I pushed the reset button on my life.

The genesis of the artist-to-lawyer transition was accompanied, oddly enough, by the squeak of a magic marker. I was at my first college art class critique, balancing my skinny frame on a metal stool, anxiously awaiting the professor's comments about a drawing I had worked on for days. The quality of the other students' drawings was daunting, but my high school teachers had heaped praise on my work, so I felt confident that the professor's comments, overall, would be positive. When the Professor reached my drawing, however, he paused, tugged on his wispy brown goatee, and pulled out the fat, black magic marker.

"Now this," he said loudly, slashing a big black X over my drawing, "is what we DON'T want to do."

Thanks to the insistence of my parents (who got remarkably smarter as I transitioned out of my teens), when I decided to switch majors, I was at a university, rather than the art school that I had argued I should attend, and I was able to parlay an English degree into admission to law school.

Law school, as it turned out, fit my talents better than art school, but the more successful I became at it, the more the pace and intensity of my life increased. I ended up at a large firm, working on multi-million dollar case for clients like General Electric Co. I was primarily the team writer, which I loved, but the harder I worked, the more responsibility I was given, and at times, the hours and pace bordered on insanity. I once remember driving through McDonalds at two a.m. for dinner, and envying, *really* envying, the heavy-set, bored woman on the other side of the window, whose main responsibility was to ask, "Do you want fries with that?"

One might think that the next turning point was accompanied by the cry of the baby, but it actually was heralded by a knock on the door. After we had our first child, I was, like many professional women, dismayed to find that Mary Poppins did not drop down my chimney. The real-life child care choices were deeply disappointing, and the time I was able to spend with my child was much too limited. My firm graciously agreed to allow me to work part time, but I found that the type of work I was doing couldn't be done—or at least, done right—in a limited, set time frame. After half a year of working full time for half-pay, I returned to being "all in." When I became pregnant with our second child, my fantasies of staying home became increasingly vivid, but they seemed economically unfeasible, particularly after my husband decided to give up his construction business and go to medical school.

The knock on the door came as we were finishing renovations on a crumbling, turn-of-the century stone house. My husband's construction company sign was still in the front yard, and when I opened the door, a perky, stiff-haired real estate agent asked if our house was for sale, explaining that she had a client who was looking for a house in this area. I shifted the three-year old child perched on my hip, adjusted my protruding pregnancy bulge, and asked, "What's your client's price range?"

When she told me, I replied without missing a beat, "Yes. Yes it is."

Selling the house made it financially feasible for me to stay home while my husband was in medical school. We moved into a small rental house, and the pace of my life went from cheetah to caterpillar. We sometimes spent entire mornings just splashing in the puddle of our short, cracked driveway. Despite my colleagues' dire warnings of boredom, I loved being home with the kids, and I hoped to stay home for many years to come.

The next trigger for change arrived silently, in the form of a letter. We had just moved to North Carolina for my husband's residency, and the public school in our neighborhood wrote to inform us that, based on my husband's salary, with three children, we qualified for reduced-price lunches at the school cafeteria. That day, I dug out my résumé, dusted off my pumps, and pulled out my pinstriped suits. This time, I was lucky enough to find a position working part-time, in-house for a corporation. For decades, I juggled work and children's activities more or less successfully. Sometimes I dropped the ball in one area or the other, and sometimes I had to stay up until midnight to get everything done, but I felt like I was on track. My life's route was set. I could set the cruise control and quit trying to plan the next turn.

Then, last spring, came an image on a sonogram. It was a dark, sharp-bordered spot inside my left breast, accompanied by the words, "I think we should do a biopsy." Priorities abruptly changed. I had been dismayed by the sags and jelly-skin that had increased with age, but I had found solace in the belief that my hair and my chest still seemed to be hanging on to a more youthful (or at least pre-fifty) look. Both were sacrificed without hesitation, to increase my odds of eradicating the cancer. Piles of "to do" lists, for the next weeks and months, were simply set aside. Dozens of seemingly essential tasks that *had* to be done by me were done by others, or simply left undone.

In the year since my diagnosis, reconstructive surgery has done a nice job of making me look normal again, my hair has recovered (in a short, oddly-curly way) from the eight rounds of chemo, and my prognosis remains good. But my sense of priorities, and my perspective, will never be the same. I appreciate my family and friends much more acutely; I savor the sunsets more fully; I gaze at the stars with more wonder. Rather than just saying, "I'd like to do that someday," I try to say, "Let's do that *now*." I used to feel like I owned my life; that it was a book I could keep forever, and read whenever I found the time. Now it seems more akin to a library book, checked out for a limited time. I am just trying to enjoy as much of it as I can, while I have it in my possession.

Reality Orientation

Barbara Seagle

Looking back on my life choices, they seem complex and amusing. It is as if I had been in a maze without any idea of how to reach the exit but had to make one choice and then another and another. There is some irony that I am a pediatrician who has spent the better part of my life helping children through their own maze, and yet I find it so difficult explaining my own.

My parents had their first date on December 7, 1941, the day Japan attacked Pearl Harbor. My Dad enlisted in the Marine Corps, became a lieutenant, and was wounded on Okinawa in 1945. He was awarded the Silver Star for his bravery. I cannot imagine doing what he did, but perhaps I have inherited some of his courage. After the war, my parents married. My Dad became an advertising executive, working long hours and traveling frequently while my Mom stayed home and raised three children. I was the oldest, the only girl, and was expected to do well in school, behave, and eventually become decorative and desirable. I loved horses and rode and did some showing. I was also a competitive swimmer.

My Mom did not have an easy time raising us with my Dad often absent. My two younger brothers had severe asthma with frequent exacerbations. In the '50s, the treatment for asthma was quite primitive: theophylline (a caffeine relative that helps open airways) and steroids. I remember watching helplessly as my brother, lying on a steamy bathroom floor, struggled for air. My Mom, desperately trying to keep him breathing, bent over him as the rescue squad pounded up our stairs. It took me years to figure out the connection between this image, forever burned into my memory, and my career in pediatrics. Perhaps I never wanted to feel that helpless again.

When I left home for college in Ohio in 1966, I began to find my own voice and had some first glimpses of my path, though it was still well hidden in the underbrush. The Kent State Massacre, when four students were shot and killed by the Ohio National Guard during a war protest, occurred during my senior year. I became politically aware, marched against the Vietnam War, and met my future husband. After I graduated with a degree in English, I moved to Boston. When my husband and I married, I was twenty-three and pregnant with our first child. This situation was viewed as ruinous by my parents, but our daughter Jessica opened up our lives, and theirs, in ways we never could have anticipated.

My husband Jamie and I had two more children. Both boys, they were delivered at home with the help of midwives. We decided on home births because of the high rates of what we believed to be unnecessary interventions (fetal scalp monitors, caesarian sections) at the hospital and because of our faith in the integrity of my body and the birthing process. We had a local ambulance service, called Bridge Over Troubled Waters (how '70s is that?!), available for emergencies. I loved caring for my babies. Never in my life have I felt as completely competent and sure of my instincts as I did then. Though I did not know it then, my path was opening before me.

As the children grew, my interest in midwifery expanded. I wanted to find a career and began by taking courses at Boston University to prepare for applying to training programs. My Introductory Biology professor took me aside one day, complimented me on my performance in class, and asked about my goals. He encouraged me to consider applying to medical school. This was a surprise! To become a physician was a goal beyond my imagination, but I had reached a point of confidence in myself that allowed me to consider this as a real alternative.

I entered Boston University School of Medicine in 1983 at age thirty-five. My younger son had just begun kindergarten. I look back now and wonder how I did it. One answer is that my husband never showed a flicker of doubt that this was a good idea. Not to say that we didn't struggle as a family during this time, but we shared this improbable goal completely. We just kept moving forward, even if the steps sometimes felt painful and laborious. I discovered my inner student and surprised myself: I graduated fifth in my class and was chosen as graduation speaker. To my delight, I matched at Children's Hospital, Boston, to train in pediatrics.

The training was rigorous, caring for the sickest children with the most advanced techniques available. I was mentored by outstanding clinicians and developed the necessary clinical instincts to observe, treat, and care for patients. When my residency ended I started my practice in primary care pediatrics. After a final harrowing night on call at the Children's ICU on the morning of July 1, 1990, I went directly to my new office to see my first patients. My partner and I started our own practice in 1993 and were together for more than twenty-one years before my recent decision to retire.

There have been many bumps in this journey. My children have provided me with a full measure of both angst and joy. They have been complicated and challenging each in their own way, mirroring the struggles parents have shared with me at the office. My husband has had a series of significant health scares: cancer, a heart attack. And primary care medicine has undergone an enormous change during my career: Algorithms, outcome measures, electronic records all have contributed to a decline in time spent with patients and intimacy in the doctor-patient relationship. Much healing occurs within this relationship. For twenty-one years my partner and I kept our commitment to practice "old school" despite the pressures. However, this was becoming increasingly difficult and disheartening for me.

I can look back and see that I have been lucky more than I have been wise. Meeting my husband, now of forty-three years, has been a stroke of good fortune beyond compare, though we have been through some tough times along the way. While not a straight shot, my children are healthy, functioning adults and have given us more than we could have dreamed, including five wonderful grandchildren. There were so many times I felt that I was blundering and making a wreck of things, but at this moment, I have found my peace. I am thankful.

Sometimes our words come back at us, and right now I am hearing the advice I have given first-time parents in what I call "reality orientation." There they sit, exhausted, exhilarated with overwhelming love, determined to not make any parenting mistakes. They never tell me this, but I see it. I've been there. I tell them, "You are not going to raise the first perfect human. Give up now." No path is perfect; no decision is beyond question. So I counsel, "Love well, be strong, laugh often, be bold, and don't think too hard." As I enter retirement, the same goes for me. And so I will.

An Unhurried Life

Deborah Mead

For many people, the years after college are filled with excitement, but in my twenties, I felt truly lost. I watched as friends and fellow alumni proceeded on career paths that seemed so purposeful. They knew where they wanted to go and did what was needed to get there. They seemed energized by striving—their crammed appointment calendars, their endless responsibilities. I tried for a time to emulate them, but it only left me feeling inadequate and miserable, drained by life in the working world.

It was only when I stepped off the nine-to-five career path to stay at home with my new baby that I realized the road everyone else is on is not the one for me. The maddening rush of the modern world—to catch the commuter train, to get to the nine a.m. meeting, to defrost dinner in time for soccer practice—doesn't suit my temperament. To me, rushing feels purposeless, my energy and sanity dissipated before the day has scarcely begun.

In the years since I left work, I've learned to embrace my actual nature, my preferred pace, rather than struggling to be someone I'm not. My truest, most authentic self emerges in quiet moments—walking in the forest with my dog or picking my daughter up from school and hearing about her day. Along the path of discovering myself, I also discovered a love of poetry, both reading and writing it. I've published short stories and poems in journals as well as in a volume of poetry co-authored with two other women. The moments of success have been fun, but the greater pleasure by far lies in the creative process, in the simple act of arranging words on a page.

I structure my day in a way that's meaningful to me, rising before dawn to put in some writing time before other responsibilities intervene. I'll write in my journal and read some poems from a favorite author—Ellen Bryant Voigt is my current inspiration—before settling in to my own work. My latest project is a collection of poems focusing on my father's final years after his stroke. In choosing to live an unhurried life, I was able to spend large amounts of time with him during those difficult years. I wrote poetry about our time together, one of which is shared below. I hope to send the collection out to publishers in the next six months, but I have no boss and no deadline. When the poems are ready to go, they'll go.

My daughter is older now, old enough for me to return to the workforce, but why would I want to? I've been asked if I get bored staying at home. People who enjoy a more driven life can't conceive of finding satisfaction in my admittedly small world. But I do, a great deal of it. Every day I find fulfillment, and every day I'm grateful for the opportunity to live at the pace that suits my temperament and interests. And if I hadn't taken the time off to raise my daughter, I might have completely missed out on discovering who I am.

Day One

That was the worst of it

not the failure of the clot buster
or the daily degradations to follow

but that first moment, looking up to find him
looking at me across the restaurant table
with eyes of expectation as if
he'd asked a question or made a joke,
was waiting for my reply

What'd you say, Dad?

The twist of the mouth
the sound that was not speech
and the look that continued
steady, patient,
full of good humor,
the moment I knew catastrophe
had quietly happened to him

and he did not

Cushioning My Landing

Melissa Ludtke

It's the clanging machine I remember most, as though hundreds of fingers were tapping typewriter keys in unison. I was at my bank, about two blocks from the mid Manhattan's Time Life building where I worked as a reporter, and this machine was imprinting the amount of a bi-weekly deposit, adding it to my others. My dad, a finance professor, had urged me to start this account when I called to tell him about being hired as a reporter at *Sports Illustrated*. "Now," he'd said, "Don't wait." When the envelope with that first paycheck landed in my inbox, I carried it two blocks to this bank and did as he'd said. Each payday, my lunchtime routine was the same, and only when the clanging ceased did I feel confident that the small amount I'd asked the teller to put into my account was safely tucked away. When direct deposit made these bi-monthly bank visits unnecessary, I missed the clanging's sense of certainty. The pounding of keys and inky scent of new numbers on my passbook's page were what transformed my dad's advice into my lifetime habit.

Looking in the rear-view mirror of the four intervening decades, it might seem odd that a mundane, routine moment like this stares back so vividly. Then again, this ingrained habit is what had steered me off of roads most taken and landed me on more scenic ones. The rides are bumpier, but my journeys and destinations have been rewarding. Let me be clear: savings I've accumulated would not purchase the longed-for lifestyle of a long-time professional nor match the perceived needs that many Americans have in entering the receding decades of their lives. For me, they are more of a cushion, there to pad my landings, not big nor firm enough to save me from a calamitous fall, but enough to prop me up while I stir cups of meaning and purpose into my evolving recipe of life.

At two junctures, one recent, the other nearly two decades ago, I stepped off usual paths to head toward places neither customary ambition nor conventional wisdom would suggest I go. The earlier detour brought me to motherhood, on my own at the age of forty-six, when I had no job. That's when I adopted a nine-month old baby girl in China. It was the life I'd always wanted, and one I figured I'd have someday. But as I built up career credentials, that day never arrived. In those earlier years, I had good paying jobs but lacked other key ingredients—a solid marriage or a like-minded partner. I'd agonized for years in my mid-to late thirties whether I could do this on my own. Then, cautionary thinking circled me back to the internal message: "Don't do it." Yet, in my late thirties, emotion took over where my rational calculations left off, and I tried to get pregnant at a doctor's office using donor sperm. My adverse reaction to fertility drugs stopped me after months of trying. My response: I locked up emotion and hid the key.

Five years later, eight tiny words exploded that lock. "So you've decided not to be a mother," my friend said. She knew I'd tried, failed, and walked away from my effort to get pregnant. I'd given her no clue to make her suspect I was done trying. Jolted, I replied, "No, I haven't." Somehow the words spilled out of me before I could catch them. I was surprised to hear them. Still, they said what I felt. Soon, my friend was handing me a slip of paper with a phone number of a single woman who'd just returned from adopting her baby in China. That night, I called her, and the next morning I phoned China Adoption with Love, an adoption agency. One year later, almost to that day, I was holding my daughter at the orphanage in Changzhou, China. My cushion was what took me to China, and it was what floated us until a terrific job found me. Then, my direct deposit, bi-monthly paycheck took over.

Sixteen years later I am absorbing bumps on another back road. With my daughter about to head to college, and still raising her on my own, journeys of a different kind beckon. Each offers me what a paycheck never could—the gift of giving back. In my early sixties now, the notion of pairing lifelong skills and experiences with the hope of inspiring others has great appeal. I'm writing a narrative history from the 1970s for those not alive when women took to the streets to demand equal rights. The part I played during those tumultuous years as a baseball reporter challenging Major League Baseball in a federal courtroom is a story I feel compelled to pass down. I'd been denied access to players' locker rooms—access my male colleagues had and I needed to do my job for *Sports Illustrated.* Judicial application of my Fourteenth Amendment rights provided remedy. Though a fair number of younger women and men have heard about this case—with its notorious intersection of male sports and nudity (think locker rooms) and "liberated" women—I can add invaluable insights, nuance, and dimension about an era and movement that frames their lives today.

For now, that book project simmers on a back burner. I stir it often enough so I'll be able to serve it on the fortieth anniversary of my lawsuit, a few years away. But what's grabbing fuller attention these days is a new adventure of producing a digital book called *Touching Home in China: in search of missing girlhoods.* For an old print journalist, making a "transmedia" iBook—meshing video, slideshows, interactive maps, informational graphics, and text to tell the story—is a surefire way to keep my mind young, since I need to learn how to do what I do as I'm doing it.

So why trade a steady job for our pared-down life courtesy of my tiny monthly pension from Time Inc. and Social Security that I took at the age of sixty-two, against the advice of financial experts? This decision circles back to the leap I took to adopt my daughter, which showed me I could and gave me confidence that things do work out. And with that adoption came our family's forever connection with China. Giving back in this realm of our life has become a habit—through my longtime board service Families with Children from China (FCC) New England, in our donations to Chinese orphanages, and in editing (in my spare time) the FCC journal *China Connection* for adoptive families.

Now, I get to give back in a wholly different way—and *with* my daughter, reason enough to push forward as I am. For the story of *Touching Home in China* is about a first-of-its-kind journey that she and her orphanage crib neighbor and friend took when they were sixteen years old to the farming towns where they were abandoned as newborns. There, they befriended girls from those towns who might have been their childhood friends and learned about girlhoods they never had the chance to live. It's a story that's never been told and one it's my privilege to try and share globally.

Can I do it? We'll see. It's intended launch is in September 2015, twenty years after then First Lady Hillary Clinton declared in Beijing: "Women's rights are human rights." On some days when I might doubt the wisdom of trying to do this, words arrive that buoy me. Recently, our filmmaker in China, the woman I hired to videotape the girls' rare encounters, wrote to me after she spent time with Mengping, one of the Chinese girls that my daughter got to know in her rural hometown.

"Mengping gave me goosebumps. What a life-changing experience your project has been for her. She said before we met in 2013, she never considered leaving Changzhou. Now her dream is to go to Japan, and if she can America, and see the world. She said she wanted an English name from us because she considers us (you?) to be her English-speaking mothers.

"What you have brought to these girls is IMMENSE."

While her words aren't jolting, as my friend's were nearly twenty years ago, they are enough to act as shock-absorbers along my bumpy road. For now, that's enough.

At My Pace (Take 2)

Jill Ebstein

I failed the first time I tried to write my story. I think I had too much to say—sort of like a carbonated beverage that has been shaken and is ready to explode at mere opening. So here is take two and I will start with a seminal moment that changed my journey.

I was working at a startup that on a good day was crazy but still productive. It was 2001, and except for me, the senior team was all men. In many ways, I stood out—from not being invited to join in the daily lunch ritual to not ending the day with drinks at a bar. They were nice enough, but I didn't really belong. One afternoon, I got a call from my nanny that she couldn't pick up the kids from school. My husband was unavailable, so I immediately left work but got stuck in a traffic jam caused by a Bill Clinton visit to Boston. I ended up being very late to retrieve my kids. There they were, ages eleven, nine, and six sitting happily at the curbside of the school, playing word games ("twenty questions" was a favorite), no worse for the wear. Not so for me. I was irritated by the late call, struggling with traffic and Boston drivers, and wondering what I got out of my job that made this complicated straddle worthwhile.

That moment gave me the push to start my own business—something I had occasionally dreamt about but previously lacked the courage to attempt. I had been on a fairly conservative and predictable path which went something like this: business school, management consulting, CitiCorp, Hewlett Packard, sprinkle in three kids over five years, capped off by a few smaller, less mainstream businesses that made going solo not so scary.

Once before, I had ventured outside the conventional career path. In 1989, after the birth of my first child, I asked Hewlett Packard (HP) to let me work part time. But back then, even the progressive culture of HP did not have a policy to easily accommodate what seemed to me like a simple request. Just as I prepared to strike out on my own, the HR department decided to try a six-month pilot program with no guarantees. That pilot lasted ten years and four bosses, and opened the door for more women like me.

I am now in my fourteenth year of solo consulting. During that time I have asked myself whether I have regrets about the path I've chosen, especially given the discussion surrounding *Lean In* by Sheryl Sandberg. While I have sometimes fantasized about the high-powered positions of some of my colleagues, I am content with my choices. I have been blessed to see and hear my kids race to the fridge, plopping down their backpacks after a long school day. I've caught them on their time, not mine, when they've wanted to share something. For this reason, and for the value I place on independence, I have consistently and with appreciation said, "No thanks," when clients have offered me permanent positions.

Of course this doesn't mean that I haven't felt the pressures of having to both hunt down and deliver on the work, keep my clients happy, meet other needs in my life, and still squeeze in some tennis and dog walks. I've won some measure of freedom and control, but I've also had to go the extra mile, sometimes with extreme fatigue, in ways I wouldn't have otherwise known. This year, for example, I got a call from a client regarding a time-sensitive engagement connected to an acquisition right before Thanksgiving. Suddenly, my holiday preparations took on new levels of complexity, but I didn't even for a minute consider saying, "No" or "Can it wait?" I said, and continue to say, "Yes" because I value my clients, and because the busy moments always get balanced with the occasional slowdowns. I compare this to a truism from tennis, where the worst thing I can do is to admire my shot. Better to split-step and prepare for the ball coming back.

What has driven my journey? I offer two data points and a dream that has fueled me. First the data points: On my desk sits a card my mother gave me fifteen years ago that shows a swing and a sky with stars and says, "A mother helps you push your swing so you can touch the stars." I also remember my Bubbie (grandmother) who at sixteen emigrated from Russia to marry a man she had never met tell me, with wonder, "I hear that in this country, girls can become a *lererke* (Yiddish for teachers.)" I watched my mom work beside my dad in our family-run grocery store while raising six children. These two women somehow subliminally programmed me to both push a swing and drive a career. I knew at a young age that some version of a *lererke* would be in my future.

Now for my dream: I have a passion not easily tamed, and that is my love of writing. At HP, as the organization grew increasingly complex, born by the pressures of globalization, and the speed of the Internet, I began to draft a book titled *Little Fish, Big Ponds*. I wanted to empower individual contributors to make an impact without depending on their overbooked manager by creating a framework for asking the right questions and then drilling down. It was the start of a self-help book. While I found an agent and engaged a publisher, ultimately they decided that I lacked "a platform," and so that book died. I hope to pick up my pen and continue with similar efforts.

Pushing my swing to the stars has meant many things. It has meant freedom, growth, family, and dreams still to come. To quote a favorite poet of mine, "I have miles to go before I sleep." At my pace, of course.

A Few Minor Repairs

Sandra Serio Gregory

I grew up the oldest of four in a slightly crazy tight-knit Italian/Polish family from Chicago. My parents were each the first-borns in their families. Perhaps being the first of two firsts explains my determination and perseverance. Add to that, I'm a Leo, which explains the rest. To me, life has always been a great adventure where I can't help but get involved. My tendency to be at life's center also meant I grew up to a chorus from my siblings of the famous '70s line from Jan Brady: "Marsha, Marsha, Marsha."

I thankfully and intentionally took advantage of the opportunities available to me and tripped the "light fantastic" through high school and college. I studied abroad in Mexico and Italy, married, and had a career as a graphic designer. By my thirties, we were raising two adorable little boys.

Go Big or Go Home
My husband and I were YUPPIES, then DINKS, and quickly

scaled the corporate ladder. I grew a busy design business that thrived through five corporate relocation moves. In 1997, we put down roots in Denver. Like many people in the '90, we surfed the dot-com wave. As a result, we acquired the requisite large house, ski condo, clothes, cars, travel and lots and lots of stuff. We gave back to our community. We controlled our world. We had all the answers. We had plans … big plans.

Then the wave crashed.

When the planes hit the towers and the economy went bust, my husband was forced to commute to a job in Florida. It was a tough time for all of us, but like so many corporate employees, time apart from the family had become the reality. After two years of weekly back and forth, the grueling commute began to take its toll on all of us. We decided that in order for him to stay around, he would explore the idea of starting his own business.

Fixing cars?
We opened five "boutique" automotive repair shops in two years. Within five years, we closed down three of those five. The company soon went belly up. We never made a penny. The partners, the decisions, the growth, and the employees, the car business itself—everything was wrong.

During that time, I woke up every morning with a pit in my stomach. I was swept up in some kind of manic energy in a business I shouldn't have been part of, in a life I had grown to hate. In the meantime, my husband was battling his own demons. We lost control of our life, our finances, and our future. I'm not sure what was to blame for our marriage going south. Perhaps it was a combination of a lot of things: A dose of ignorance, a heaping spoonful of arrogance, gallons of booze, plus a dash of bad luck. The recipe for one colossal fuckup.

Chapter 2: The 50,000 mile tune up

It didn't take five years in the car business to quickly realize I needed a few minor repairs. My first decision: "Have less so I can do more." When I listed our home, I ordered an 8' X 8' X 8' storage POD. What fit into that POD went with me to my next life. The rest was left to history.

After our home sold, my brother and his family kindly invited my youngest son and me to stay with them. As a lanky high school junior, he needed the privacy of the guest bedroom. This left the basement to me. There I was: fifty years old and sleeping in my little brother's basement on my niece's Little Mermaid big-girl bed.

Oh, Marsha, Marsha, Marsha!

There, snug in my underground cocoon, wrapped in my pink and purple Ariel comforter, feet hanging over the end of the bed, I simply simplified. I sipped my morning coffee (ok, and a few evening wines) and made myself sit and just … sit. At first, of course, it was a sloppy pity party: "So that's it? He left ME? No big house? No big husband? One big fat failure?" I had to literally force myself to be OK with the idea that this was my reality. But the more I just sat, the more I became OK with the idea that for now good enough was just … good enough.

A whole new world. A new fantastic point of view …

It didn't take that long to realize it was time to get on with it. I posed the questions I needed to help figure out: What was next? As my Excel spreadsheet bucket list evolved, *travel* became a recurrent theme. In reality, I just wanted to run away from home. Regardless of the motivation, however, it was time to get back on the road. But I was broke. So of course, I needed to be *paid* to travel.

So I Googled: "*Be paid to travel.*"

… and a few things came up:

Teaching English as a Foreign Language. *Not for me.*
Importing or Exporting. *Maybe.*
Hopping over to Italy to see about George Clooney. *I'll keep that one in my back pocket.*
Tour Director. *Well, now you're talking!*

There were three places in the world you could get certified as an International Tour Director: The Netherlands, San Francisco, and *Denver.* The stars were beginning to align.

For months after I completed my certification, I was consumed with applying for jobs, researching countries, and setting my course. Stunned and blinking, I finally emerged from the basement into the sunlight with a new job as a Tour Director. The future was becoming brighter. I was scheduled to go to Italy in February.

Also in February, my divorce became final. When the gavel fell to end our twenty-three years of marriage, my new ex and I stood out in the corridor trying to come up with the words to say. What I realized at that moment was: I didn't have to say anything. I didn't have to make my point. We didn't have to rehash who did what to whom. It didn't matter. The boys were really okay. We all were going to be fine. Not perfect. Just fine. All I said was, "I gotta go." And just like that, I drove away from that courthouse, from that man who was so much of my history, and I hopped on a plane to my first tour of Italy.

So what have I learned from all this?

I've learned you don't have to go big or go home. My grand plan is not as important as getting up every day and being happy with the little wins. I'm starting my sixth season leading tours and have also started my own tour company, Che Bella Tours. My life now is a whirlwind of attending to guests, maneuvering motor coaches, confirming hotels, in-depth commentary, stand up comedy and a lot of "I'll be happy to take care of that for you." Typical days include thirty thousand steps on my Fit Bit, great wine, bad airports, unexpected treats, and every color of security level advisory out there. And I love it.

I've learned how to be present and listen. On tour, you are not simply a guide, but also a friend, a confidant, and sometimes a kind of therapist. I take a sincere interest in every person who comes into my life. I have learned how to play close attention sit and listen closely to what they have to say. Watch carefully what they do. Understand them as a person. And learn from them.

I've learned to believe in soul mates. I truly became the person I was supposed to be after the gavel fell. What I thought was the lowest point of my life was actually a rebirth. My world has become an odd, magical adventure. I now live in the Caribbean, take people on vacation for a living, and as of this writing, am planning a sunset wedding to a kind, wonderful man who totally gets me.

Before I left for my first tour, my Mother Outlaw told me in her thick Kentucky accent, "Saaandy, shit happens. But you're going to work in Italy. The only thing you really need to say is, '*Graziaaay*!'"

This past summer, while I was gazing at the Pantheon for about the hundredth time, a beautifully dressed Italian woman wandered over and stood next to me. After a moment, she leaned over and said, "I like that song too." I was humming "Somewhere Over the Rainbow". Because I was over the rainbow, grateful and happy. *Si, grazie mille.*

Creating My Own Show

Evelyn Starr

My story is one of trial and error. And of achieving my dreams in ways I could not have imagined even ten years ago.

As a child, my father Harvey regaled me with tales of his days at the office. He would arrive from his commute out of New York City to our suburban New Jersey home each night at six o'clock. After he changed out of his business suit, we would chat for a few minutes before dinner. Each of Dad's stories came with an insight.

"What comes after the decimal point on an interest rate matters."

"Reward employees who show initiative."

"Don't tap a secretary on the shoulder to get her attention."

It was like going to the Harvey Starr School of Business. I liked it. I wanted to go into business and rise to the top of a company like Dad. When I was eight years old I declared that I was going to be President of IBM and buy a house with a tennis court for him and my mother. "Great," said Dad. "I can't wait to retire."

When I was fifteen, I discovered the joy of writing and the benefits of keeping a diary, thanks to a gold and white dime-store journal that my brother gave me for Hanukkah. I chronicled events, confided worries, worked out solutions, and dreamt of one day being a writer—after my corporate career, of course.

The beginning of my career path went mostly as planned: I earned a Bachelor's Degree, worked for three years, got my MBA and landed one corporate job. Then another.

The first inkling that maybe my career was not to be a straight upward trajectory came about two years into my job as Marketing Research Manager for Dunkin' Donuts. I had been in marketing research for seven years and was looking to try something new. I knew I had to make the jump to a position with revenue responsibility if I wanted to achieve my dream, which had evolved to becoming Chief Marketing Officer somewhere.

The Director of Beverages considered me for Coffee Product Manager but could not get over the fact that I did not drink coffee. (I could see her point but believed I could have done the job anyway.) I attempted to create a New Product Manager position that would be heavily research-based, but I failed to persuade the Vice President of Marketing to separate the responsibility of managing *new* products as a job in itself.

Meanwhile, the Director of Marketing Research position opened up. Though I raised my hand for the position, the company opted to go with someone who had more years of experience. Despite her greater years of experience, her subject matter expertise mirrored my own, and I was not learning anything new from her. My professional development came to a halt.

So when I had my son, I opted not to return from maternity leave. I figured I knew much about marketing research and nothing about motherhood. When my son began sleeping through the night, though, I caught myself trying to optimize the spacing of feedings and to analyze other aspects of caring for my son which were really straightforward.

After a year I went back to work, before anyone got hurt. At The First Years, a company that marketed infant and toddler products, I got the New Product Manager position I had wanted. They saw a marketing research professional with a one-year-old as a New Product Manager who came with her own test market!

In concept, the fit was great. In practice, it was a disaster. My tolerance for long meetings that management mistook for productivity went from its waning status at Dunkin' to zero. I kept thinking I could be getting something done or be with my son.

The CEO valued face time heavily and patrolled the halls at nine o'clock in the morning and six o'clock at night, taking a visual roll call. With a toddler, I was out the door to daycare pick-up at five o'clock, with my heart racing as I dashed to get to there before closing. I was exhausted, and had little energy for my husband and son.

One day a freelance copywriter I worked with complimented my writing. We had been working together on package copy and instruction manuals and she liked my editorial suggestions. She encouraged me to think about becoming a copywriter myself. I liked the idea and imagined that I might go out on my own years later in my forties.

Instead, I did it two months later. It was the only option that appealed.

Full-time motherhood hadn't worked. Returning to a full-time corporate marketing job hadn't worked. My research told me that even if I was lucky enough to get a part-time job, I would either get a sideline role (less important projects, little professional development) or a full-time role masquerading as part-time (part-time pay for full-time aggravation).

So I followed the Hollywood model. With no desirable roles in front of me, I created my own show. I hung my shingle out for marketing research, marketing strategy, and copywriting.

It was November 1999, and I was two months pregnant with my second child. My plan was to spend my pregnancy networking, take a six-month maternity leave, and then try to parlay the networked contacts into work.

I got a client in my eighth month. I bought one enormous black suit for an interview and then worked from home for Gillette for the last two months of my pregnancy. After my maternity leave, Gillette hired me for another dozen projects before they were acquired by P&G.

Over time, I started working for smaller clients where the projects allowed me to play a more strategic role and to write for them.

Eight years after I started my company, my husband decided he wanted to create his own show too. He asked me to help start his company. Who knew that my chance to create and build a brand from scratch, and to be a Chief Marketing Officer, would come from my best friend in life? I am happy to report his company is strong and growing in its seventh year.

Three years ago, in an effort to generate more leads for my business, I started a monthly marketing newsletter. At the time I did not grasp how gratifying this marketing tactic would be. Instead of waiting until after my business career was over, I was now self-publishing and being read by hundreds of people each month. Soon more people were hiring me to write newsletters, web copy, and other marketing materials for them.

So today I am head of my own company of one, the behind-the-scenes Chief Marketing Officer of my husband's company, and writing on a regular basis. It's not how I originally envisioned my career path, but the quality of life benefits have made it better than I could have imagined.

Finding My Voice

Ellen Arad

Before I ever uttered a note, I knew I could sing. I felt it in my soul. But for what seems like forever, it was a well-guarded secret. You see, I was raised in a home with two very high profile women, who could also sing. My mother was a coloratura soprano with the NYC Opera Company back in the forties. Her ill health kept her from realizing her potential, her dream. My older sister had a one-time offer to sign with a record label when she was a teenager, but a clash of personalities rendered the deal null and void. Suffice it to say, from a tender age, embedded in my subconscious was the feeling that I could not succeed where they had not. And so I stilled my voice, and opted instead for academic excellence.

Subconsciously, though, I kept looking for subtle, non-threatening ways to develop my voice; in college I began to take vocal instruction, and in graduate school I produced and starred in an original rock opera written by a fellow student. Later, as a young career woman, I hovered around the arts. I worked as an associate producer for *Good Morning America*, and a story editor for Punch Productions, Dustin Hoffman's production company, while pursuing a Masters degree in communications from NYU. On the eve of graduation, my professor and advisor took me to dinner, and offered me a doctoral fellowship. I was thrilled, but nevertheless had to decline; I was engaged and moving to London in six months' time. They agreed to keep the offer on the table for two years, and should I return within that time frame, the fellowship was mine. We returned to New York five years later, long past the sell-by date of the fellowship.

The years in London were challenging ones. I thought that with my credentials and work experience, I'd be welcomed by the media community. But in '80s London, women in media were a miniscule percentage of the work force. I rode the length and breadth of the tube, going on interviews, to no avail.

When we finally moved back to the States, I'd been out of the work force for nearly five years. We had a newborn and I didn't really want to jump back into the frenetic world of live television, and so I had to start from scratch. I became a freelance feature writer for an entertainment industry monthly paper. Once again I found myself drawn to a career that was tangential to the arts, using my voice to highlight the work and creativity of others. It left me restless and unfulfilled.

Until one evening when a knock on the front door created a whole new path. The woman who was the family educator at our synagogue had come to inquire whether I'd like to take over the monthly children's service. Although I had no formal training, I was quite game to give it a try, and poof! I became a Jewish educator. Within six months I had created enough demand for the service to go from monthly to weekly, and I became the music teacher not only in my own synagogue, but also in several others throughout the county.

In my third year of this new career, I branched out by teaching older children in religious school, as well as adults. It wasn't glamorous—it didn't quite have the cache of *Good Morning America*—but it afforded me the opportunity to be present for my children, and for my parents, who were ailing, and had become increasingly dependent upon me.

I was the poster child for the sandwich generation, experiencing the challenge of caring for young children and infirmed parents while still in my thirties. Still, this new track inspired me to return to graduate school for a Masters in Jewish Education. I wanted the credentials necessary to call myself a Jewish educator. There we were, my children and I, sitting at the kitchen table, all doing our homework. Those memories are precious and lasting.

In my classroom, music was my tool of choice for instruction, my guitar my constant companion. While pursuing this Masters, I studied privately with my childhood cantor. I wanted to learn cantillation, the art of reading from the Torah, and how to be a service leader. I considered these skills necessary for any professional Jewish educator, and unfortunately, weren't included in the curriculum.

Early in the process, my cantor encouraged me to enroll in cantorial school. He even had the Dean call me. With great reluctance, and some trepidation, I began pursuing my third Masters degree, as a *hazzan* (cantor). When I embarked on this leg of my journey, I had no intention of pursuing a career as a cantor, mostly because a career would likely mean moving elsewhere to serve a congregation, and my family was rooted in New York. The closer I came to completion, the louder the voice inside me grew. "You can do this," it said. "Find a way."

As my career as a *hazzan* continues to unfold, I realize I am still finding my voice. The voice that I use as an agent for the congregation on Yom Kippur, the holiest day of the Jewish year, is not the same voice I use as a chaplain to bring comfort to a dying patient. The voices of an artist on the concert stage, or of a teacher in the classroom, are different still. Just recently it occurred to me that while I don't have a traditional pulpit, I have still managed to shape my cantorate and encompass almost every facet of the profession in my own way and on my own terms. I believe this to be unique in the cantorate, but so perfectly fitting for my personality. Never one to follow a traditional recipe, I like to add my own spice. As for my personal cantorate, well that recipe isn't quite finished, but I am looking forward to see what happens next.

Discovering My Way

Fran Eichholz Heller

I love my job, but it has not always been that way. I am a social worker in palliative care at Columbia Presbyterian Hospital. With the help of a talented team, I try to ease patients' pain and, when appropriate, help them achieve a peaceful end-of-life. I landed here through a series of steps and missteps, calculations and serendipity, and a few seminal moments that paved the way.

From the start, when I was young my family traveled for extended periods to Spain and Mexico while my Dad was on sabbatical. I developed excellent Spanish language skills, and more importantly, an awareness of other cultures and norms. This early exposure helped plant a seed for building connections beyond my local zone. It probably helps explain the immense satisfaction I receive today as a go-between for Latinos trying to make their way through the complex American medical system.

I had some early detours in my journey that were also critical in shaping me. After college, I went to work doing PR for an art book publisher and later helped fundraise for the ACLU. They both upped my skills and professional network but left me longing to contribute in a way that I had yet been unable.

During that period of confusion and self-doubt, I thought back to an early childhood moment when Sergeant Shriver had announced the formation of the Peace Corps. I was a mere five years old at the time, and told my parents, "I want to do that." While it took a professional void to refocus, I eventually joined the Peace Corps. I was in my twenties, and went with my husband to an isolated community in Ecuador. My husband introduced new agricultural techniques and crops, while I taught nutrition, maternal childcare, and first aid. It was a perfect job, but alas we came back to the States to start our family.

If joining the Peace Corps was the fulfillment of a long-held dream, returning to the States was open and unscripted. When we began our family, I wanted to stay home. I joked that it was more for my personal development, than it was for the kids'. They were halcyon times. I was part of a cadre of college-educated moms with little money, but we were all in it together with playgroups, co-op babysitting, and the like. But after six years and money being tight, it was time to return to work.

Wanting flexibility, I decided to start my own travel business. I tapped into my connections in publishing and became an agent for authors' book tours. Through a relative, I expanded to Wall Street and served an environmental brokerage firm called Nat-Source. It turns out that flexibility was more important than I had ever imagined as my daughter became ill and eventually lost her fight with cancer. I spent countless hours at Sloane Kettering, working on my laptop at her bedside. My sad world became sadder when my marriage completely came apart. About my only consolation was the decision I had made long ago to stay home during my children's early years.

After my daughter died, I continued with my travel business. My Wall Street client, NatSource, was an energy brokerage that traded green house credits to industrial polluters looking to offset their carbon emissions. This was 1998 and they were ahead of their time working in a pre-compliance market. At one point, I shared my opinion that they were missing an opportunity by not selling energy credits to the retail market to help environmentally minded individuals offset their own carbon footprints.

After my daughter's death, Natsource's CEO approached me about whether I wanted to take my retail idea and run with it. When I heard the words, "I want you to be in charge," I thought, "Why not?" I have often emboldened myself with a belief that being afraid to do something is never an excuse not to, and so I said yes. There I was, situated on the trading floor, which felt more like a frat house than a business environment. It was a good experience, but after two years, I realized that something like the Peace Corps was much closer to who I am. Another checkmark for self-knowledge, but where would I find fulfillment?

Then one day, serendipity hit. I was having coffee with an acquaintance who happened to be a social worker. As she described her job, a light bulb went off. I remembered when I was living in the hospital caring for my daughter, and I would often serve as translator for Spanish-speaking families. I so enjoyed being useful and providing support. When I returned home from coffee, I announced to my second husband, "I want to quit my job and go to social work school." His response to my new calling was short and sweet: "Go for it."

At the ripe age of forty-four, I enrolled in grad school. I was one of the oldest in the group and considered every day an opportunity, no matter the workload. My first day was on 9-11, and I was at my internship at a Senior Center in Washington Heights. There were many Latinos in the room with me, glued to the TV, some of them political refugees that had fled to the US as their ultimate safe haven. Their doubt and anxiety were palpable. I was in the right place for me.

While my goal at the outset of grad school was to serve in palliative care, it took a while for that to happen. It was a nascent field, and the opportunities were few. My Spanish language skills were key to being hired. I've now been at Columbia eleven years and have watched the team grow with a full complement of professionals, fellows, residents, and interns.

We also continue to innovate. Recently, we were able to begin collaborating with clinicians in the Dominican Republic (DR) in response to our patients' wishes that they return home for their last days on earth. After five trips to the DR to administer training, I feel that I have come full circle in integrating my love of Spanish and my desire to serve. The twists and turns along the way have made it all the sweeter.

Not Surprising

Judy Elkin

"What's your best day at work?" my coach asked me. It was our second appointment, and I was trying to decide if I should stay at my dream job at Brandeis running a graduate program to prepare Jewish day school teachers or leave ... and do what? I had no idea! I told my coach that my best day is when I meet one-on-one with students, help them figure out their workload, or their relationship with their mentor, or best yet, their career path. If we proceed to their relationship with their significant other ... jackpot! We both looked at each other in a knowing way. I want to do what you do!

It's been eight years since that ground breaking process and I now work full time as a life coach, helping others navigate career transitions. At Brandeis, I retooled myself and gained certifications through The Coaches Training Institute and The Center for Right Relationship. Symbolically and pragmatically, I then morphed the room in my home that mirrored the many phases of my life—first a playroom, then a piano room, then a storage room, and now, a warm and welcoming office. In this comfy abode, I greet my clients either face-to-face or on the phone. I often walk into my office, minutes after blow drying my hair and making a cup of coffee, to engage with my first client of the day. I feel an overwhelming sense of gratitude for the life I've been able to create.

This career path is not that surprising to those who know me well. I was always the therapist to my family and friends growing up. For some reason becoming a therapist just didn't occur to me when I graduated college. I had wanted to be an English teacher but instead went into Jewish education, inspired by various mentors in my life. One job led to another.

When I became a mom of three kids, my priorities changed, and I was fortunate to be able to work part time in this field during their young years. Then the dream job at Brandeis appeared. I will never forget the transition as I went from a full, yet spacious, life to a life on steroids. The learning curve and adrenaline rush expanded my hours to be way more than full time.

The decision to leave Brandeis happened in two stages. First, with the help of my coach, I redefined my job and adjusted my perspective, enabling me to stay three more years. During that time I started to slowly build a practice, albeit with some ambivalence. In the second stage, I worked part time while I determined if I could really make a go of this new career. After one month it was eminently clear to me that I needed to make a complete move. I wanted to develop my expertise as a coach, and I needed the time and space to focus. During this evolution, I was calmer, happier, and despite all the anxiety of being a neophyte, I was more confident.

Now, if you were to ask me to describe my best day, I'd say it's working with five or six clients a day, helping them envision and give shape to their career path or life stage. It's about giving people permission to make a change that will give their lives more meaning. Almost every client says the same thing when they first connect with me. They want to do something that matters.

Take for example Michelle (not her real name) who came as a last ditch effort to stem the extreme burn out she was experiencing working at Booz Allen in a very senior position. She was in her late thirties, married with two young kids she hardly saw, and making a ton of money ... and she was miserable. Through the coaching process, Michelle gave voice to a passion for aesthetics and creating workable and welcoming spaces for people that would bring out their best. When she felt more secure, she admitted that she longed to be an interior designer but was too embarrassed. It didn't fit with her Ivy League background. Long story short, she also retooled, and is now blending her work with her passion as an interior designer. She made it work.

Now, when *I* ask clients "tell me about *your* best day," I listen intently for clues as to what lies ahead for them. While it's not always as immediately evident as it was for me, (and in a way for Michelle), eventually it becomes clear. And when it does, there is incredible satisfaction in knowing that I've had a part in helping them get there. It's not at all surprising to me that being that person for them is what I'm meant to do.

The Art of the Career Choice

Jeanette Kuvin Oren

I wasn't used to disobeying my parents and this was a difficult phone call: "Mom and Dad, thank you for sixteen years of great education. I am quitting my PhD so I can become a full-time artist of Judaica." I had passed my oral exams and completed eighty percent of my dissertation in psychiatric epidemiology. I was also very sure I needed to be a full-time artist. To their enormous credit, my parents—whose motto was "art is an avocation, not a vocation"—asked only one question: "Can you support yourself if, God forbid, something happened and you were left on your own?" I naively answered, "Yes!", and I've never looked back or regretted this decision. Every day I get to be creative in a field I am passionate about, meet people around the world, and be my own boss.

That phone call took place thirty years ago. Since then, I have worked with more than three hundred and fifty organizations—and hundreds of families and individuals—across the world to create Torah covers, Ark curtains, stained glass windows, large mosaic installations, paper art, wall hangings, and metal Ark doors. I work in many media (fiber art, paper, painting, glass, metal and mosaics), and all of my work is commissioned. This means that I am hired by the organization or individual based on my previous body of work. Together, we discuss the design, themes, colors, and overall effect of the art. Then I make the art.

I learned early on that being a successful self-employed artist is less about art than about communication, confidence, and smart business choices. I began my career making commissioned *ketubot* (marriage contracts), working with couples to help them translate their love into calligraphed, painted and papercut works of art. How I do the art, however, is less important than how I listen. Do I really hear what they want and who they are? This is even more challenging when I work with committees. To get ten members of a synagogue committee to agree about what new Ark doors should look like is no easy feat. But when I truly listen, I can assimilate each person's vision into a whole. Listening, envisioning, and communicating are the best tools in my art box.

Saying "yes" to the different requests for commissioned art is almost as important as good listening skills, and can require a degree of bravery that at times tests my limits. And it is not just a simple "yes" but a yes with confidence. This was the case, for example, when I was asked to create a large mosaic for a school's lobby that would set a tone for the new building's entryway and also acknowledge their donors. I had never made a mosaic, and in this high-stakes case it would need to communicate the school's values, and thank donors in a respectful and subtle way. A very tall order indeed, but like the lion in Wizard of Oz, we often have more courage than we realize.

Lest people think that being an artist is pure fun, only thirty percent of my time is spent doing art. The rest is spent tending to the business so that I can actually have my fun. I had to decide early on exactly what type of work I would be soliciting. As appealing as retail art was (prints, greeting cards, etc.), I chose to focus on commissioned Judaica. In hindsight, this was a wise strategy that enabled me to focus on the art, my customers, and differentiated my offering from the many artists out there.

Though I am proud of my success, the journey has not been all smooth sailing. There have been some bad business choices, but obsessing over money wasted on a particular magazine ad or a bad retail outlet doesn't help anyone. We all make wrong turns along the way. Failure is part of any successful journey. The occasional stumble is how we get smarter.

It turns out that following individual passions must be a family theme. My husband, in the middle of medical school, took a year off to write a book because he became immersed in the history of Jews and Yale University. I sometimes chuckle when I think about my parents who probably breathed a sigh of relief when their impractical daughter was at least marrying someone sensible and grounded. Dan did become a physician and a researcher. As I write this, he is in Poland studying how light affects blood and therefore is key to our moods and physiology, a life-long interest of his. We are kindred souls with enough practical savvy to make it work.

I look at my daughters and think that there might be some downside to the behavior I have modeled. Unconsciously, I seem to have taught them that running your own business means flexibility, being home at any hour, loving your job, and dressing in sweats. They see no downside. This makes me nervous. Are their expectations unrealistic? My oldest daughter has loved anything to do with dogs since her first words, "See the Rhodesian Ridgeback, Mommy?!" We pushed her to finish her masters degree in education, but what she really wants to do is to make a living with the non-profit organization she founded that places rescue dogs in foster homes. She wants to leave her "safe" career as a teacher for a risky career running her new non-profit. What's my first reaction? "Could you support yourself if … ?" Then I stop myself and tell her, "Do what you feel passionate about. And do it well."

Overcoming Writer's Block

by Ellen Morton

Just who are these self-aware, self-directed people who know from a young age what they want to do with their lives? At one point, when I was about five, I wanted to grow up to be an eagle. Otherwise, I gave no further thought to my future.

I hit college (fortunately a liberal arts school) without a plan. I drifted and dabbled through potential majors, settling for a while on special education, as I liked the idea of working with kids, particularly those facing challenges. But I started feeling guilty that my parents were forking out so much money for me to learn how to design class bulletin boards, so I pulled the plug on that major.

As fate would have it, I developed a crush on the bad boy, rabble-rousing editor of the college newspaper. When he asked me to do a feature column, I gave it a whirl. I am nosy, and I loved that journalism gave me license to ask probing questions that would never come up in normal conversation. Not only would people answer my questions, but then I could put their words in print … under my byline! Lordy, it was a heady experience. It was the late '70s, the post-Watergate years, and journalists were regarded as demigods. I interned for the local paper, picked up some stringing work for the wires, and cobbled together enough credits and clips to graduate from college with what I thought was a viable clip book.

I bypassed moving back home and set out to make my mark. Where did all aspiring journalists go at that time? To Washington, DC, home to Woodward and Bernstein. It turns out my timing could not have been worse. The job market in general, and for journalists in particular, was abysmal. Knowing nobody, I found a room in a group house and started wandering the halls of the National Press Building handing out my resume. The search went on for weeks, then months. I was grateful to get a job as a parking cashier to tide me over as I persisted in my pursuit of a job, any job, that would pay me to write.

Fortunately, listed on my résumé was the line 'Stringer Reporter for the Sewickley Herald,' because it distinguished me from the dozens of others applicants vying for an editorial assistant job with a small trade group. My boss-to-be had spent some years living in my hometown, and that little line item is what got me in for an interview and helped secure me a job. For the next ten years, I was essentially a flack for various industry groups, writing newsletters and press releases and handling media relations. Not as honorable a gig as I had hoped, but writing was involved, bills were paid, and Washington, DC, was a vibrant backdrop to my twenties.

Along came a husband, a first home, a first son, and a growing realization that working full-time in go-go DC and seeing a baby during his waking hours were mutually exclusive. So we loaded up the van and moved to Arizona. My husband, Dale, took a pre-arranged job as a food microbiologist, and I started free-lancing for trade publications, covering meetings throughout the West. Another son came along, and my very capable husband and I became skilled at tag-team parenting, even handing off kids at the airport when needed. It was with great regret that I gave Dale my blessing to accept a job in Chicago, though the move, some twenty years ago, proved beneficial to us all.

Around the time the boys entered elementary school, I was approached with a dream job. A DC-based publisher wanted to hire me full-time to write and edit a couple of well-respected national newsletters. I would have a real salary, write stories with real import (at least to a specialized crowd), and I could work out of my home. It was all that I had aspired to.

I may be guilty of burying my lede, but I should mention that I hate to write. I HATE to write. Always have. My diary from my youth is filled with page after page of 'ditto.' At best I ascribe to the adage: "I hate to write, but I like to have written." Ironic, I realize, since writing was at the core of my professional life for twenty years. What ended up on the page must have passed muster, because people were paying me. But the solitary and introspective process of retreating from the world and going *mano-a-mano* with my keyboard runs directly counter with my intensely social and (okay, I'll admit it) slightly shallow personality.

The next few years in my 'dream job' were spent miserably holed up in my windowless basement office for eight or more hours a day, awaiting returned phone calls from sources that always seemed to come when I stepped out to walk the dog. As deadlines neared, a cloud of dread and doubt descended making me difficult to be around.

Those dark years in the basement coincided with the manically over-scheduled period common to any two-income family with kids of a certain age. Dale traveled a great deal, while I sat in the stands at the boys' various sporting events frantically editing stories, envious of the parents who had the luxury of catching up with each other while they cheered on their kids.

I had reached that "something's got to give" point. Fortunately, Dale was doing fine at work, and we could weather scaling back to one income. Truly the only thing standing in my way was my reluctance to give up such a good gig.

Around this time I came across a column (that I have held onto for years), written by one of my favorite *Chicago Tribune* columnists, Barbara Brotman, about a woman in a similar position. The woman executive had a fulfilling, meaningful job, but missed being with her kids. "Kids are young for such a short time. They want you in their life for such a short time." she said. "I don't want to miss this time."

My sentiments exactly.

Once I had assurances from Dale that I could keep the cleaning lady despite my unemployment, I resigned my job and threw myself into all those self-indulgent pursuits long denied: book clubs, exercise classes, movies with friends. I was present and accounted for as a mother and wife, overseeing household renovations, organizing impromptu outings, and even cooking dinners.

But as the saying goes, "Nature abhors a vacuum." I started picking up small jobs that didn't follow me home at night. True to my initial instincts in college, all dealt with education, as a classroom aide, religious schoolteacher, or substitute teacher.

I also allowed myself to get sucked into the 'volunteer vortex,' taking on tasks with ever increasing levels of responsibility. Soon I found myself serving as both president of our synagogue and of our neighborhood association, positions potentially rife with conflict and self-serving personalities. It was then I found that, unlike my writing job where I always felt a bit like a misfit, I possessed that hard-to-define, either you have it or you don't interpersonal skill that allows me to bring people together and peaceably work toward higher goals. In all likelihood, it's my intense dislike of conflict that contributes to my success as a mediator/cheerleader, but whatever, it works.

Now I'm executive director of our synagogue and a writing tutor for special needs college students. Yes, I'm lightly compensated monetarily, but well compensated in terms of impact and reward. What have I learned from my meandering path toward personal and professional fulfillment? That those jobs that seem most glamorous and lucrative take a toll if they rely on a talent you may possess but don't enjoy. That it can take decades to realize you have a unique, marketable skill that they don't teach in college. And that the bad boy you have a crush on at eighteen is nothing like the solid, capable man you fall in love with at twenty-eight. Especially if that man lets you quit your job *and* keep the cleaning lady.

On the Need to Dig

Suzanne Offit

A small white canvas pencil case with the block inscription: "I am not so much a traveler as I am an explorer," is one of my favorite gifts from my husband. Ever. I felt so heard. Much of our lives we spend trying to explain ourselves, frustrated by the limits of mere words. After twenty-eight years of marriage, this affirmation with such elegant simplicity (black and white, a small zippered case capable of holding only the most precious of transportable items) was priceless. He understood a personal drive that has been within me from the start. I am a "seeker," both energized and soothed by the search for meaning and wisdom.

The seeds of seeking were evident as a toddler. My favorite book was *A Hole is to Dig*, which still sits by my bed. As a child, I was digging into Ruth Krauss's simple wisdoms and Maurice Sendak's joyful drawings. I walked, hiked, and biked, and even then didn't calculate the distance but the depth. And I could cover great distances while standing in one place.

In my twenties I met and married Andy, and we only started to understand what a relationship could be. When our twins were born I was incredulous that I was to hand over my perfect, healthy baby boys for ritual circumcision. The tradition was clear but how could this be? My search for answers in my own Jewish tradition set into play a whole new course.

I was a young mother whose husband was often traveling. I attempted to find the holy in three small boys at home while I discovered my new found passion: Torah study. I still remember the look on Andy's face when he returned from a trip abroad and found me surrounded by boxes. "I just bought the *Encyclopedia Judaica*," I announced with unfettered glee. There I was digging into a new treasure.

Then came the tumult. The day before our third son started kindergarten, I started rabbinical school. I became subsumed by a full-time, intensive, academically challenging, spiritually deepening endeavor. Yes I did still have three kids in elementary school and a husband who worked full throttle in his profession. What was I thinking?

My day started early, before 5:30 a.m. with laundry, breakfast and lunch prep, email, and a moment to breathe for myself before I got the family up and out the door. I was so thankful for an early bus pickup so I could clean up and get to my morning prayers at 7:45 a.m. My days were filled with blissful learning in Talmud, Torah, history, law, liturgy, education, theology, and philosophy. Suddenly it would be 4:30 p.m. and I would be jolted into my alternate reality as I rushed to pick up kids and begin the evening routine of dinner, homework, and bedtime.

If lucky, I could begin studying by 9:00 p.m. and collapse into bed at 11:30 p.m. For the first three years of my six-year endeavor, I said to myself *every morning*, "This is my last day of school, I don't know how much longer I can keep going like this." Yet each day I sang a song of gratitude to myself as I backed my minivan out of my driveway to attend another day of rabbinical school.

For my kids, the kitchen table was now frequently populated with rabbinical students discussing Hebrew grammar and Talmud texts. My husband, on the other hand, was bearing the brunt of a new family schedule, increased religious observance, and limited interactions with me.

It got bad. Very bad. Fear and resentment started to emerge. There was silence and very loud conversations. The status quo was unacceptable. So, with the help of a therapist, we both began to dig and were able to find each other again. New language was introduced. We admitted, discussed, apologized, articulated needs, found common ground, and deepened our relationship. Anger was replaced with curiosity, appreciation, and ultimately love.

The sum of those six years of digging and metamorphosis taught me much more than the many parts of rabbinic education. I found my voice and my place in the history of Jewish tradition. I felt immense gratitude. Without going anywhere geographically, I was able to travel eons intellectually and spiritually, and most importantly, I found a way to take my family with me.

Posted on my refrigerator is an Anais Nin quote that says most of what you need to know about me. It reads, "I must be a mermaid, I have no fear of depths and a great fear of shallow living." The mermaid in me has plunged into deep waters and found her home.

I am now in my fifties and have proudly achieved an integrated wholeness. I am a rabbi and palliative care hospital chaplain, and I am a wife, mother, daughter, sister and friend. All. One. I believe I have found that sweet intersection defined by theologian Frederick Buechner: "The place God calls you to is the place where your deep gladness and the world's deep hunger meet."

My days are slightly different now. Less driving, more navigating. I continually explore the earth as a gardener and beekeeper. I get to read books like, *The Meaning of Human Existence* and Mary Oliver poetry.

As a palliative care chaplain I behold the soul of another human being in deep exploration as she culls her own personal depths for meaning or safety or calm or healing. I work with patients, families, doctors and nurses to help navigate the scary world of health care decision-making. I teach young nursing students The Spirituality of Care. Since I am an interfaith chaplain, I appreciate the wisdom of many religious traditions as I seek to honor the paths of all my patients.

All my exploring and seeking has led me to me.

The Consequences
of a Sweet Tooth

Rachel Miller

My career path has been somewhat unorthodox, at best. After graduating from an elite college with all of my pre-med requirements fulfilled, I decided that I didn't really want to be a physician, and so I found a hospital research position, working with like-minded and fun-loving individuals. I enjoyed the camaraderie more than the work, but it was fine. Computers were becoming mainstream, and I had dabbled enthusiastically in programming during my senior year of college. So when the hospital established its first Information Technology department a few years later, I eagerly requested a transfer. This time I enjoyed the work, and was asked to apply for a management position. But I was pregnant with my first child at the time and declined the offer. It seemed the obvious choice to me.

I was fortunate with the birth of my first child; I was able to negotiate a part-time schedule with only one day in the office and the remaining hours at home. My mother spent the one day bonding with her grandchild while I connected with my office mates. With the second child, I was just part-time at home, and with my third pregnancy, I finally acknowledged that even that was no longer feasible. On the day I finally stopped, a huge weight lifted off my shoulders. I was free to apply myself to my real full-time profession—my family.

I was always puzzled as to why mothers "had to" stay home with the kids while fathers "got to" go to work every day. As the mother of four children, now grown adults, I am the first to acknowledge that child-rearing can be demanding and challenging, but personally, I have found the rewards to more than compensate for the effort. And I have never understood why our society devalues the incredibly important job of raising our next generation. That said, I am also keenly aware of my good fortune that I didn't have to work. We could get by on one salary, which is not the norm these days.

The next few years flew by—after school activities, volunteering, household management, and even an occasional opportunity to indulge in one of my hobbies like quilting or baking. Yes, I spent a lot of time in the car chauffeuring, but it was time spent with my kids, which I knew was a limited and precious commodity. As the children grew, I began to work part-time at a nursery school during their school hours. I remember sitting at my son's basketball game and overhearing another parent say to a friend "Can you believe it? That guy went to Harvard and now he's teaching nursery school!" It took all my self-control not to turn around and say "What's wrong with that????"

I think my turning point came about ten years ago, when my oldest child reached his teenage years and asked me, "Mom, I don't get it. You worked really hard in high school and got into Harvard, but for what?" It hurt deeply, although I fully understood that he couldn't grasp the reasons for my choices at his age. Nevertheless, I began to contemplate my options for "post-motherhood."

That was a while ago. As our children left the nest and my job as mother was downsized from full-time to consultant, I decided to pursue one of my hobbies more intensively. Although I knew I couldn't replace the passion that I feel in my role as mother, I wanted to find something I loved. If you love your work, it's not work, right?

After a year of internal debate, I went to culinary school to become a pastry chef. From the moment I entered the school, I knew I had made the right choice for me. I spent hours on my feet piping profiteroles and creating genoise, but the time flew by. I checked the clock, not to see how soon I could leave, but rather, how much longer I could stay. And I loved the expression on my friends' faces when I presented them with the results of my labors.

My highly educated relatives still look at me quizzically when I tell them I'm a pastry chef. I try not to measure my success by their faces, but rather by how I feel at the end of a working day. One unexpected delight has been the pride that my grown children take in my new profession. Perhaps they're just glad that I'm gainfully employed, but I think they also appreciate my unconventional career choice. And they don't mind the leftovers, either!

The Canvas I Have Painted

Jill Kerner Schon

I vividly remember the conversation with my oldest daughter, Jackie. I was telling her about a phone call I'd had with my college friend, Shelley, in Atlanta—a call that I didn't know would change the direction of my life. Talking to Jackie that afternoon, I was lamenting my work life: as a single mom of three daughters for many years, my recent work, for one reason or another, had not materialized the way I had hoped.

I asked Jackie what she thought of an idea Shelley had shared with me. She had gone with her friends to a place where you paint and drink. I had never heard of the concept and asked her to explain it. Shelley's response: "Surely you have that in the Northeast!" Before I could argue that we did not, she took a picture of her painting and emailed it to me. Looking at the painting, I was stunned. After all, Shelley was a numbers person—good at math. I didn't think she had it in her to produce such a fine painting. "It's easy," she said. "They tell you exactly what to do."

"Wow," said Jackie, an accomplished painter, when I had finished. "That is brilliant."

Within one week, Jackie and I flew to Atlanta where we visited three paint and sip studios. Each place was packed—upwards of fifty people, all painting, drinking, and having a merry time. We returned to Boston with a strong sense of urgency that if this business were to happen, it would need to be immediate, or else it would become someone else's brainchild.

Three years later, The Paint Bar has two sites in the Greater Boston area, loyal customers, and wait lists for a packed calendar of events. Going to market quickly was essential, as we now have a number of competitors, and although we are doing well, I maintain a healthy unease. In addition, we are able to give back to the community through donations and fundraisers. A wonderful mix of family and friends, (all employed; no unpaid internships is a strongly-held value of mine), has helped create a warm, open environment.

To be clear, my journey has been anything but a straight shot. I started as a writer working for Beth Israel Hospital and John Hancock, two large Boston institutions. When Apple invented a computer that allowed me to use my eye and a mouse pad to do graphic design—and with young children at home to care for—new possibilities emerged, and I went solo. I was married at the time and didn't need either a predictable income or health benefits. My divorce, however, created new, daunting realities that turned me back into an employee. When I learned about the paint-and-drink idea, I knew my daughter and I had to go for it.

"Going for it" was not easy. I had very little money. Our town had few available liquor licenses. And then there was our combined background—strong on art and weak on business. Looking for funding proved nearly impossible as bankers dismissed everything—me, the business idea, even my home equity. I understood their response. It was a similar response to that of my accountant and my closest friends, all of whom would have performed intervention if they thought there was any chance of success. The constant refrains went something like, "Southerners are different than us," "This isn't the way we do fun," and, finally, "You don't have the money to gamble." No matter, I was going forward.

I was able to borrow the needed start-up money from two friends and hired a lawyer whose expertise was getting liquor licenses approved. The night of the town meeting, as the committee ruled on my application, the room was flooded with friends, my rabbi, and even my former mother-in-law. They may not have understood my decision, but they were still with me all the way.

Shortly thereafter, The Paint Bar was launched. The first event was the fiftieth birthday celebration of one of my closest friends. It was written up in the local newspaper and, a short time later, we were featured on the local TV news magazine, *Chronicle.* Unbeknownst to us, a happy customer had sent them a letter. *Chronicle* stirred a lot of interest. Good thing, too, as I was going to have to dip into my reserve to pay the next month's rent!

While it sounds like we've landed the plane, there are looming issues ahead. More competition exists, and we have to be concerned about it. We wonder if we should expand to a third Greater Boston location or more fully maximize the space we already have. And it is no longer just the two of us in the business—we have a staff of about twenty people to manage, including my second daughter, Mia.

I have sought help through an unlikely mentor: Zingerman's Deli in Ann Arbor, MI. They, too, have loyal customers and have expanded their brand, all while staying true to themselves.

So with seeming success after an entrepreneurial leap, why did I just redo my basement? An employee of ours lives there now, but should our business go off course—as indeed my life once did following my divorce—I would still have a comfortable place to live. I have what I call a "you never know" kind of life. We all do. We just don't always know it.

By the Numbers (and Not)

Anonymous

Many adjectives can describe me: intense, analytical, and passionate, but today, maybe my favorite is "work-in-progress." I have been in the investment business for over twenty-five years. When I was nineteen years old, I decided I wanted to be an investment banker. Why an investment banker? Maybe because it was the '80s, and I was a Wharton undergrad, and it seemed so exciting to be in the middle of high finance and deals that made the news. Maybe because I was nineteen and didn't really know what I wanted or what motivated me. All I knew was that I loved the pace of investment banking—working with really smart people, meeting CEOs, staying up all night, getting dinner at the office, and enjoying the intellectual challenge of deciphering a company's value.

All was going according to plan. At twenty-three, I got engaged and returned to Wharton for an MBA. Upon graduation, and with significant effort, we found a city that offered opportunities for both our careers. I accepted a job on the buy-side for a large Boston based mutual fund company, which suited my passion for investing in distressed and bankrupt companies. The job required analytics, attention to detail, pouring through legal documents (it fascinates me for some reason), and arguing with people about a particular deal (another odd pleasure of mine). Mostly, I enjoyed rolling up my sleeves and actually helping the company change its strategic position and future outlook.

The rhythm to my life was working well, and then I had my first child. After maternity leave, I went back full time, five days a week and said "yes" to everything: late nights at the office and a summer spent commuting to London every other week while I had a six-month-old at home. Before being a Mom, I would have probably thought that traveling across the pond was exciting but in my new reality, I was annoyed and considered it a test.

My hunch was confirmed, when one day a portfolio manager insisted I go to Australia for a two-day trip to analyze a very small position. I was seven and a half months pregnant and my first baby came early. More than forty-eight hours of travel for two days of work? Did they expect me to deliver on the plane? When I called my doctor, he laughed at its absurdity and offered to write a note saying I couldn't go. I declined the offer because I considered myself too old to need a Doctor's note for something patently obvious. Instead, I simply refused to go.

When I was invited to join a firm started by a few of the portfolio managers I had worked with, I eagerly went. Shortly into my new stint, I discovered how much I enjoyed being part of starting a business and realized that I liked a smaller, more personal firm.

There was ample opportunity to learn, grow, and see your impact. Eventually though, the business matured, and I got restless. Start-ups were now officially in my blood, and so I moved on to help start another asset management firm. This happened two more times in a fifteen year period in what can best be described as "start-up fever."

My last position, though, introduced a new shock to my system and started my grand awakening. I had spent seven years trying to grow a fund in the midst of the Great Recession. It was very difficult, as I was stretched by also being chief cook and bottle washer, perhaps to the breaking point. It felt like I was nearing the "time to make a change" moment. When I received a work email with questionable ethics, I walked into the office of the head of the firm and resigned. While everyone assumed I had another job, I explained that I needed time to decompress, and maybe change things up. I am pretty sure that they didn't believe me, but it didn't matter.

It turns out that jumping off the fast track is not that hard. I began by scheduling lunches to give me a semblance of meetings. I met with a colleague, who had similarly retired, to review investment ideas and stay current. But all these efforts were sideshows to the main act, which was to find a more meaningful way to give back. It is why I enjoyed helping distressed companies. While much of my life has been about the numbers, the part that most fulfilled me was not.

Since that fateful resignation, I have joined several non-profit boards, enrolled in Jewish studies courses, travelled, learned to cook (really well!), and helped a friend's son by working to expand the programming of a school for kids with disabilities. I am also part of an angel-investing group focused on helping women entrepreneurs.

In this unscripted phase of my life, I take some satisfaction that I am beginning to figure it out. This is important not only for me, but for my family. As a Mom, I want to think I am leading by example, and in this case, it is as simple as "follow your passion." I look at my daughters who, at seventeen and nineteen, are just starting out. I chuckle that one daughter is pursuing medicine (like my husband); the other wants to pursue economics (like me), though not Wall Street (because of me).

So, even though I still cringe a little when asked, "What do you do?" I am growing more comfortable with my answer, "I am taking a gap year, or two, to figure it out." After all, the there are so many possibilities—math teacher, Rabbi, entrepreneur—and maybe the only thing they all have in common is that in different ways, they all have the potential to give back. I guess my "by the numbers" training could only take me so far.

Taking a Few Left Turns

Donna Surges Tatum

Perhaps it is that I am a Pisces. Or because Daddy got me a planetarium for Christmas when I was five and taught me about astronomy while also telling me the myths regarding the constellations projected on my bedroom ceiling. Or maybe it is just in my DNA.

I have always been a dreamer with a scientific perspective. I am logical but trust my intuition. I believe the Universe provides paths that we must perceive in order to gain our highest potential.

As a kid I rode my bike all over town. I would pedal along, see something interesting, and make a turn to go in a new direction. I was pulled to all sorts of neighborhoods where I would meet people and dogs, explore the woods, marvel at gardens, and admire the houses. Some routes were magical, some were a little scary and others were boring, but I followed the winding roads until I was home again.

Most of my life has been a combination of the quantitative and the qualitative; the spiritual and the material; the pathos and the logos. Yin and Yang.

As an incoming freshman at Purdue I knew I was going to major in English and Journalism. Then I attended my first college class, and found my home in the Communication Department. I studied the theories and applications of communication science. I loved all my courses whether they were interpersonal, interviewing, rhetoric, persuasion, organizational, or social movements. I stayed on for graduate school. It was glorious.

I was attracted to the bright lights in the big city and moved to Chicago to be an advertising account executive. I left Purdue without writing my dissertation, but I knew I could always finish when I wanted to. Meanwhile, it was exciting to use what I learned, and to learn what I didn't learn in school. It was glorious.

One day I took an information call during lunch when everyone else was out of the office. I met the potential client for lunch, and was mated by dinner. I might add that I wasn't looking for some old guy—he was twenty years my senior, although age never mattered. Jim and I had a never-ending conversation for our entire thirty years of marriage. It was glorious.

I have the soul of a teacher. A friend from graduate school was teaching part-time at Roosevelt University, and moving on. He suggested I replace him. Thus started an eight-year love affair. I taught students who ranged in age from eighteen to eighty. Roosevelt is a vital urban institution whose mission is to provide education to anyone who wants to be given the chance to prove ready to learn.

When I was named to a three-year term as chair of Roosevelt's Communication Studies Department, that pesky PhD reared its ugly head. We drove to Purdue. Jim looked for housing while I talked to the department. Devastating news—some of my course work was too old, and it was going to take longer than a year to complete requirements and write my dissertation.

On the way back, Jim said, "You know, we have a world-class institution in our back yard." I had never considered the University of Chicago because they did not have a Communication program. A new path was beginning to appear.

I took classes in the business school. Although I liked the coursework, it didn't feel right. Then I found the Cognition and Communication program. The "Communication" in the title was not related to the field of communication I had previously studied; this program was psycholinguistics. But I enjoyed the material and continued to take classes. When I took a class in Creativity, we were asked to devise a way to test a mathematical model of creativity. I conceived a study to look at creativity in public speaking. When I implemented it, I ended up with a stack of data and no clue how to make sense of it. Someone told me to go see the leading proponent and pioneer of Rasch Measurement, Ben Wright, in the MESA (Measurement, Evaluation, Statistical Analysis) department. So I crossed the Midway and found my way home ... again.

"Home" because nobody says, "I want to be a psychometrician when I grow up." Yet somehow that is what happened to me. I ended up completing my doctorate in the MESA department. Now I tell stories with numbers as well as words. I get to do curious things like look at sixty-six ways of cooking McDonald's french fries to ensure customer satisfaction.

I own a business, Meaningful Measurement, in an esoteric field where I work with organizations to maintain standards in the high-stakes arena of board certification and licensure examinations. So areas like Alzheimer's care, psychiatric rehabilitation and physician specialties are held under scrutiny and measured many times over. Although I still teach communication, it is on a part-time basis at the University of Chicago. I followed the paths as I perceived them and ended up in a place both familiar and foreign.

As I reflect on the myriad paths that have been available, I realize there are some lessons that can only be learned by choosing the "wrong" one. I continue to explore new routes because I believe that is one of the great gifts we have while we are here on this earth. It is a journey, and we have the joys of both planning and spontaneity while we travel. It is up to us to be sensitive to what is offered, and to at least occasionally take a left turn.

Channeling My Energy and Dreaming Big

Natalie Goldfein

I like the truism, "The past is no predictor of the future." Every investor knows that line. Good teachers know it at some level when they try to jumpstart their under-performing students. For me personally, it is an accurate description of the twists and turns of my journey—one that sometimes surprises even me, and I've lived it.

Early on, I was an educator, and I did it well. I worked with others to create engaging programs. I taught both kids and adults, and through these efforts, felt the satisfaction of helping to strengthen communities. I come from a family of educators and so teaching felt as natural as brushing my teeth. While not one to seek the moral high ground, I liked the feeling that I was contributing to society and helping the next generation.

At some point, I was rewarded for my efforts with a new job that brought scale and took my responsibilities to a whole new level. I was suddenly responsible for a project of three foundations and doling out a great deal of money. It was both heady and weighty. I couldn't believe that I was in a position to make these calls; the repercussions felt heavy. The pace of my new job was thrilling, depleting, and mostly unsustainable.

I can look back at that period and marvel at how good I looked on the outside. I was thin, working out daily while reading the paper and shopping online—a model of efficiency! My outside looked hot, and my inside was a mess. Crazy hours, playing hard, pushing my body to the limit. And then one day, I woke up and just knew that this had to end. I needed something that was gentler on my soul, and still left me feeling that I was making a positive impact. It was as simple as I needed to feel good inside, too.

And so I began my search. It sort of sounds like a children's tale. First I found a stranger (aka, "coach") who could help me. Then I went to the bookstore to relax in the stacks and see what inspired me. The bookstore was named "Transitions," which described exactly where I was emotionally. I was ready to open myself up to alternative ways of experiencing my world. The first new class was about *chakras*—the study of the energy sources of the body; I was intrigued

When I entered Transitions, that itself was a statement. Previously, I had been intimidated by the place which seemed to specialize in spiritual development. Was it a cult? Who were the people who frequented this shop? What would this say about me? But once there, it was like being inside a big cookie jar with so many tempting ways to go. While there, I found a small unimpressive handout, announcing a class called Psychic U, taught by Sonia Choquette.

Next thing I knew, I had registered for the course and was going to develop my psychic muscles and see where this experience would take me. So began my journey into personal energy and vibration. In short order, it became my passion and explained so much about how we interact with others, how we feel, what we create. I began to recognize that there is power in what we put out there beyond what I had considered before, and I called it "Inspiring Energy."

With the inspiration of these new learning experiences, reading and working with many people, I became focused on the idea of how we harness our personal energy to improve ourselves and create happier, more impactful lives. I needed techniques that would become part of my daily living, which, if successful, I could impart to others. I wanted to figure out a way to provide an opportunity for people who weren't necessarily interested in going on retreats, reading extensively, or taking long courses to improve their lives. "How do we help them?" I asked myself.

Just as ideas were blossoming, my mother was diagnosed MCI (mild cognitive impairment) that would eventually become full blown Alzheimer's. This emerging reality rocked my world. I come from a close and loving family, and we were "all in" to care for my Mom and support my Dad. Life happens, plans get derailed, and I became the critical point person. Managing the care and supporting my family meant that other priorities were cast aside.

My Mom died on February 2, 2013. That year was a total blur. I had little structure, no energy, and was in deep mourning. I didn't fight it, I just lived it. Eleven months after her passing, I awoke with renewed energy and focus. It was palpable and after I waited a few days to make sure the feeling didn't pass, I began my first steps in creating a new business: My Habit Upgrade.

My Habit Upgrade is a reflection of my journey and my goals ahead. Besides being educators, my family also has a history of entrepreneurship, and that page in my book has just begun. I want to contribute to the way people feel, function, and fulfill their lives. To some, this will sound kooky. To others, way too soft. But for me, it is as simple as using techniques to improve our energy vibration.

Through the use of a website, My Habit Upgrade will provide a personalized approach to self-improvement. While the past is no predictor of the future, the path I've charted will combine all that is meaningful to me, and has been since my beginning: joyful learning, self-improvement, simplicity, challenge, and entrepreneurship. I am mindful of the path I've chosen and believe that whatever beauty I possess will be far more than skin deep.

Farm Forward: Planning for a Sustainable Retirement

Gretchen Dock

When you grow up on a farm, it's hard to get beyond certain memories: the early morning smell of coffee perking; getting dressed and going to the barn to feed the animals; doing barnyard chores after school and on weekends. My mother used to say, "Roots grow deep." And this was especially true as I began to plan my retirement four years ago. I wanted to return to the farm.

Of course, if you had told me when I was a teenager that I would be retiring to a farm, I would have suggested you go for a heavy dose of counseling! How could I even consider returning to the hard, physical labor—and all that dirt?

The advantage of growing up on a working farm is that you get exposed to all sorts of critical issues from the start. Like life and death. We had Morgan horses, a few milking cows, and chickens from time to time. We experienced the joy of watching animals being born. We grieved the death of stillborn calves and watched in horror as a horse died of tetanus. We also had numerous farm cats and dogs, and we quickly appreciated the wisdom of keeping all our animals safe from mishaps and predators.

My parents were well-suited for farm work. Having served as a Navy Seabee in WWII, my father was physically strong and preferred hard labor to sitting in front of the television. He was a plumber by trade, mechanically inclined, and a natural negotiator, which enabled him to renovate our farm, fix all sorts of machinery and barter for everything. Fortunately for all of us (including the animals), my mother was a registered nurse who quickly identified symptoms that would become problems if left untreated. She and my grandmother were also excellent cooks who routinely baked goods for neighbors. Over time, I acquired an appreciation for generosity and a knack for communication and collaboration. After graduating from high school, I packed up my bags and moved to the city to attend college—taking with me the powerful lessons I had learned from my folks on the farm.

I took advantage of city living (and cheap rent) for the better part of twenty years as I worked through the changing landscape of my professional career. I began as a teacher, which taught me everlasting respect for people who do this for a lifetime. After seven years, I switched to marketing communications in small technology companies that prospered and were acquired, teaching me the value of stock options. I was then invited to be a partner in a marketing consultancy where we worked with technology companies that were facing a crisis—from resignations and layoffs to reorganizations and acquisitions. As a marketing SWAT team, my colleagues and I worked onsite with client teams to fix what was broken while interviewing and hiring our replacements. It was a counterintuitive business model, but it worked like a charm as long as we had the right consultants: people with an adaptable mix of skills, strength, passion, persistence, listening, and leadership. After three years we were acquired by a large agency. This event set the stage for retirement planning and buying a condo with my partner in a four-unit brownstone.

During the fifteen years that we owned the condo, we oversaw the management of building repairs and finances. We learned a lot about the workings of a property, inside and out, and came to understand the costs of deferred maintenance. On our watch, the building required a new roof, a new furnace, new washers and dryers, new gutters, gas pipes and lighting fixtures, and much more. Our condo was also in need of repair with new kitchen counters and appliances, ten new windows, installation of central air conditioning, a new spiral staircase to the roof deck, and gallons of paint. All of these projects enabled us to establish a tight working relationship with select carpenters, plumbers, electricians, painters, and repair people. Just like my marketing consultancy, we needed to hire the right people—then listen and lead in a flexible manner. We learned that providers prefer to be paid on the day they finish their work, and when we did this we found a very responsive crew.

In our final years at the condo, we joined a local community garden to re-familiarize ourselves with gardening. My childhood farm had many acres and multiple gardens, so I relished the arrival of fresh veggies and flowers in our small garden plot. Then we began to fantasize about how much we could grow with more property and a bigger garden. One conversation led to another, and we were suddenly talking seriously about the possibility of retiring to a farm. We shared our vision with our financial planner, and he applied his due diligence to affirm that our dreams were viable. In 2011 we sold the condo, and eighteen months later, we closed on our farm.

Unlike the farm I grew up on in Maine, our retirement farm in central Massachusetts capitalizes on advancements in materials and technology—and benefits from our lifelong experiences. We spent our first year working on major renovations at our farm, and we thought nothing of it because of our firsthand involvement with renovations in our condo building. Our retirement farm functions as a modern-day community, expanding and contracting to accommodate invited friends and family members. We have several gardens and continue to expand our growing area into the field beyond the house. Our retirement farmhouse also accommodates an aging population. Since we are not spring chickens, we thought of creating a disability-friendly house from the start—making sure the first floor is easily accessible for elders who may be sporting canes, walkers, or wheelchairs. We also sought out a property that already included a bathroom, bedroom, and laundry facilities on the first floor.

Looking to the future, I'm sure time will continue to teach us numerous lessons. My Mom had it right. Plant those roots to grow deep. But the real key to success is planning when, where, and how to plant them. My partner and I believe we have done just that in our farm community.

The Long Road Back

Marla Choslovsky

My youth was shaped by images of The Women's Movement—photos of bra burning in *Time Magazine*, *Glamour* magazine articles on having a career and what to wear for it, Title IX in the newspaper. In my own family, the esteemed one was my aunt who had six children in the '50s and '60s before going back to school to become a lawyer and judge. My aunts who had two or three children and worked in traditional female jobs (teachers, secretary) merited little discussion. And my own mother, who was home with four children, one with extreme special needs, often voiced low self-value about being a stay-at-home mom. All of these influences shaped my vision of a career trajectory.

But when our first child came along, the urge to stay home was so strong that before my maternity leave was over, I had submitted my resignation at work. I was surprised that my husband was in complete agreement, because we had met in business school and because he'd grown up watching his mom work in the family business. For the two years leading up to my resignation, we'd banked most of my salary, living on only my husband's paycheck. This financial cushion allowed me the freedom to stay home.

At first I took it one year at a time, and every year there was a reason to delay returning to work. Two more children came along, and my husband's firm grew to the point that we didn't need the second income. Meanwhile, plenty of meaningful volunteer opportunities filled my time. Before I knew it, seventeen years had flown by. I could see that when the older two left for college, I'd be able to go back to work without disrupting our household. It would take two more years before I actually did go back, but the wheels were turning.

As I talked to friends, the feedback I consistently received was, "You're so smart and you've done so much. You'll have no trouble going back to work." But it didn't take long to realize that skills and worthy volunteer experience weren't enough. I'd been out of the work force so long that nobody was going to think of me and call me in for an interview. I had to put myself out there. Around that time, a friend of mine co-authored *Back on The Career Track: A Guide for Stay-at-Home Moms Who Want to Return to Work*. I didn't agree with everything in the book, but it was enough to move me to action. The first step was to create bandwidth to take on a new major responsibility, which meant saying no to new volunteer tasks and winding down existing ones.

A self-assessment led to the quick conclusion that the engineering and computer programming track I had once been on wasn't something I was in a position to pursue now. Those skills had lapsed and that world had changed beyond recognition, for the better. (I remember lugging a bulky, twenty-pound Compaq 486 computer through Newark Airport while wearing high heels, as compared to traveling with a laptop, roller bag, and stylish flats today.) I no longer fit in that world, nor did I want to. Even if I did, I couldn't compete with the newly minted professionals in those fields.

At the same time, my communication and strategic skills had grown considerably, and in my volunteer work I had gained two decades of experience in fundraising and development. Without too much head scratching, I identified development as a career I could transition into. In this growing field that requires no specific academic training, with plenty of interesting organizations in Boston (my city), I was able to present an appealing résumé and get interviews. The difficulty came in finding the right match and in having the courage to remove myself from consideration when the job wasn't right, even though my ego would have liked a job offer.

I found my transition job by networking—essentially, talking to everyone, all the time. One day, entering a *shiva* house (a Jewish house of mourning), I ran into a mom I knew from Little League. I told her I was looking to go back to work and wanted to take her to coffee and pick her brain for an hour about the development work she does. Her jaw dropped. She said she had an opening she needed to fill immediately and to call her at the office. That chance encounter led to a three-days-a-week job administering a philanthropic grant, a one-year position that led to an offer of a permanent position (which I declined).

Once in the workforce, potential future employers didn't view me as a risk the way they had when I was applying as a stay-at-home mom. So in my second job search in as many years, I could focus on finding a good fit. As I write this, I've just completed my first year in that job.

These days, I look at life through two juxtaposed views. The first is of my own children, ages twenty-two, twenty, and fifteen, as they start on their own career paths, the decisions they are confronted with, and the visions they have about how their lives will unfold. The second is of how I got to where I am today, both the path and the outcome quite different from what I envisioned when I was their ages. Both perspectives serve a purpose. We need a feeling of certainty in order to formulate a plan and start along a path. At the same time we must be open to what we find along the path, including forks, rest stops, detours, newly paved sections that let us speed ahead, things we learn along the way, other people on their own journeys.

I don't know what the next fifteen years will hold, but I do know it's enough time to make a significant contribution.

Having It All—
Just Not All at Once!

Anonymous

I never wanted to have it all. I only really wanted to have a career. Enrolling in a college class, "Women in Business" (yes, it was a long time ago) gave me the opportunity to meet women in the business world. One day a woman came to our class; she was the vice president of a large bank. She carried a beautiful briefcase. Her career sounded exciting and fulfilling, and when she left, I knew I really wanted to carry a briefcase.

Right out of college, I started my career selling mainframe computer systems (got to carry my briefcase!) and then moved to a marketing position at a competing computer manufacturer. I spent twelve fulfilling years learning product marketing and management, moved up the ranks to a worldwide marketing manager position, and exceeded my wildest dreams of success in the corporate world. I loved my career and the people I worked with.

I met my husband early in my career and moved from one coast to the other to begin our partnership. We were both very interested in a career life and agreed that we would probably not have children. It was the '80s and life as yuppies was fun and exciting. We bought our first home, took great vacations and worked, worked, worked. Five years into our marriage we had a casual conversation about having kids. I don't know why we never thought of it before, but all of a sudden the pursuit of a career only life seemed to be missing something. I was so certain (in hindsight mistakenly) that having children would not be *that* much of an interruption to my career.

With our first two babies, it seemed like I could manage it all. I took short maternity leaves and was happy to be a mom and have my career. Home-based childcare allowed my continued traveling to Europe and across the US. My husband was traveling worldwide, and it was all working out just fine. But then things got tricky. I was scheduled to go to a management meeting in Hong Kong while my husband was scheduled to be in Europe. Something started to feel wrong. Neither of us would be on the same continent as our babies. We wanted to have a third child, and I started to question if I could handle it emotionally and practically.

At this very time our financial situation changed dramatically, the result of my husband's professional success. What happens when a person (mother) "no longer *has* to work?" It's a question I've pondered many times. The sacrifices of career/home life balance are viewed from a different perspective. When there is a financial necessity, people make do and figure it out. When you have a choice to not be on a plane to Europe while your children have strep throat and your nanny calls in sick—that's a harder choice. It's a very individual decision and I knew what was right for me and for our family.

I see women judged harshly both ways: Why does she work? Why did she quit? We need to be true to ourselves and respect every woman's choice.

We had our third child, and I worked on a reduced schedule for another year. We then moved the family across country and I officially retired from corporate life. It was a bittersweet goodbye to the eighteen-year career I loved. My identity had been my professional life and I knew I would miss that, but I was also excited and optimistic about the future.

I threw myself into the volunteer and philanthropic world. I joined non-profit boards, volunteered at schools, was a Girl Scout leader for ten years, became involved in local politics and school funding initiatives, helped raise millions of dollars for many different organizations. My favorite volunteer jobs were the ones that felt like a business. I ran the school lunch program at our elementary school—revenues doubled, profits rose forty-five percent our market share was eighty-seven percent! OK, we were feeding the kids burritos and pizza, not the healthiest of choices I admit, but I squeaked every penny out of that program, and the funds helped the school build a garden, improve a library, and provide more science and arts for the kids. I had a great time running that silly lunch program. I used all the skills and managerial experience gained from my career in my community service.

My life for these eighteen years was fulfilling and challenging in so many ways. I enjoyed our family life and feel so fortunate

I had that time with our children and my husband. I took care of myself spending time with friends, competing in sports, and enjoying outdoor adventures.

Last year with our youngest finishing high school, some new ideas started sprouting in my mind. I missed the business world, the world of customers, products and marketing issues. It just felt like it was time to start another new phase in my life. Although I had been away for a long time, I've started exploring opportunities to engage again. It's been fun to reunite with old colleagues, meet new young professionals, and learn about a business world that has changed dramatically. My career won't pick up anywhere near where it left off, my goal is less defined (one goal is to attend meetings where I don't have to provide snacks), and my work will look very different from traditional corporate life. The uncertainty of it all is scary but exciting. Call it a gap year, a sabbatical, or hiatus—I'm taking time to think about how I want to spend my time and begin my next act.

I'm comfortable with life in stages, or phases, or acts. It's exciting and rejuvenating to launch into a new phase, and it's also satisfying to close a phase and build on the lessons and skills learned. There's a theory that our greatest regrets are for the things we didn't do, not the things we did. I've tried to live my life with this in mind, and as choices and decisions present themselves, I always think ahead to the tradeoffs. Life is full of tradeoffs. It's hard to predict if you'll regret a decision, but experience helps develop an inner voice that seems pretty reliable. I have no regrets for my eighteen-year career off-ramp. I'm so grateful for my family and I know how fortunate I am to have had choices. I now look forward to the next chapter of my life.

III. Women in Their 70s and 80s

The Corner of My Blackboard

Jane Marilyn Bette Cropp Jamison

I have spent most of my life finding worthy outlets for my excess energy and enthusiasm. It is a life pursuit, and it still surprises some that at eighty-four, I have not succumbed to a "let it be" mentality. I can tell that my daughter has some mix of pride and concern, as she calls me daily on her way to work, to see how I am. I live in western New York and Ellen lives in Chicago, so we keep tabs by phone mostly. She always starts the conversation the same way: "Hi! What do you have going on today?"

What she usually gets back is something like, "I am going to a board meeting for the Institute, and then I am helping Betty balance her checkbook. Hopefully everything will be on time because I need to drive a lovely woman to an eye doctor appointment in Wellsville." Ellen's response is usually something like, "No potluck gathering today?" Well, sometimes I can fit that in too, but only sometimes.

As a former teacher, I am fond of questions, so the question I ask myself is, "What makes me this way?" In today's parlance, people call it "being all in." It does not come from a fear of missing out. Rather, it is a desire to give of myself. This quality I attribute to my upbringing. I was born in New York City and spent my early years living in a residential hotel in Manhattan. During the summers, I escaped to a beautiful rural camp in Litchfield County, CT, where my mother worked in the camp office, and my father served as the on-site handyman on weekends. They led a life of working and giving—some to their children, but a vast amount to people we didn't really know.

My parents' work ethic and civic duty was one of their greatest gifts to me—even more than the summer camp they made possible. At a young age, I accompanied my mom to a World War II service center to help sort supplies and pack care boxes for soldiers. My dad organized visits to wounded soldiers in the city's hospitals and also participated in food and holiday gift drives. As a family, we were "all in," and their actions said more than any words could have.

As it turns out, I was school smart. I skipped two grades and finished high school at the tender age of sixteen. It was not in the cards for me to venture far, but a parent's friend told us about Alfred University, a small school in rural New York, with an engineering program. I was strong in math and dreamed of pursuing engineering until I realized that there were no women in the field.

With women in engineering as a null set, I thought it would be difficult to find a job when I graduated, so I chose a more conventional route and became a math teacher. I stayed in the field of numbers and hoped I could transmit my passion to the next generation. College provided me not only a livelihood but my life partner, too, as there I met Irwin, a local boy from the neighboring town of Hornell. He had similar values, served in the army, worked hard, and when he finished duty, we returned to Hornell. There we raised three children while he ran his parents' clothing store and I began my teaching career.

I was twenty-eight years old when I entered Hornell High School as a geometry and pre-calculus teacher. I had great expectations for what my students could achieve, even if for many, their formal education would stop when they finished high school. For some, learning was easy and natural. For others, each day was a struggle. I tried to make math fun and used unorthodox approaches like showing the movie *Donald in Mathemagic Land*. I approached my classes with the same perspective that I used on my own children. Math was important, but even more were the lessons about life itself. Hence, my favorite spot was on the corner of my blackboard where I would write the saying of the day. For example, "Say what you mean. Mean what you say," could inspire a great classroom exchange. Eventually we would proceed to solving math problems.

In the '80s, personal computing hit, and I fell in love with Apple computers. I saw their products as vehicles to enhance and in some cases actually enable learning. I was asked to teach computers and eventually developed the curriculum for the school district. I became the first secretary for the New York State Association for Computers and Technology in Education (NYSCATE—a name longer than my own! Even after I retired from teaching, I continued to build the NYSCATE organization well into the '90s.

When retirement came, I chose many options, all of them great. I substitute taught, joined the library and hospital boards, and volunteered as a literacy tutor. The last sparked a new flame: serving underprivileged community members. It began with helping someone balance a checkbook, and then I realized the bigger challenges for this population revolved around navigating the safety net of social service programs. My work expanded to arranging dentist visits, trips to the V.A., and actually driving people to their specialist appointments.

In the course of serving the community, I happened upon two agencies that coordinate services, and now I volunteer with them three or four times weekly. The giveback to me is greater than anything I provide to them, and though I was honored recently with a "Spirit of Volunteerism" award, the recognition is really beside the point. I feel a need to write on some blackboard, "This is what happens when you take your heart along with you."

An Unpredictable Path

Lee Gardenswartz

I knew I was one of those people who beat to a different drum when I graduated college and did not pursue, as my friends did, a "Mrs. degree." It turns out that the passion inside me was about education and inclusion, and so upon graduating college, I ventured west to teach English to middle school students in Los Angeles.

It was a long stint—fifteen years in the LA school system—the last chunk of which was particularly unique and laid the groundwork for an unpredictable next chapter. I was teaching the likes of Emerson and Thoreau and having a fantastic time of it, when I was approached to partake in an experiment aimed at kids who were at risk for dropping out. This would require my giving up a job that I knew I enjoyed to pioneer something totally new to me. After considerable thought and consultation, I accepted the challenge, albeit reluctantly.

The experiment was ahead of its time and involved establishing an alternative setting for kids who were not succeeding in a traditional environment. The district secured a home, and we established some basic rules. Daily, students had to spend some time reading, and for this we created a comfortable lounge. They also had to dedicate themselves to an interest—for example, repairing cars—and we would build upon that. They had to show up on time, be responsible, relate to their peers, and by the way, if they hadn't eaten breakfast, make themselves something before their day started. We had a kitchen for that.

Our team provided "learning" in the largest sense. Instead of just teaching literature as I was trained to do, we also worked on building essential life skills. I didn't know that this experience would serve as a kind of Petri dish for what lay ahead. After two years in the job, I was asked to leave the classroom and help the school district prepare communities for mandatory bussing.

The project was dubbed "Project Change" and involved managing cultural and attitudinal change at the most visceral level. I worked with a colleague who would later become my future business partner. The resistance, volatility, and community unrest that Anita and I experienced remains unrivalled to this day.

Little did I realize that my need to help the disenfranchised and build an environment of inclusion would take me to a whole other world. After many years and positions in the school district, I left with Anita to spread the gospel of inclusion to businesses. This actually wasn't about preaching. It was about developing the tools and framework that would help those so inclined to build an accepting and nurturing environment. The endeavor was fraught with risk. After all, we were educators, not business people, and the learning curve would be steep.

We started by doing something we knew best: writing. We reasoned that while we knew little about marketing, we could probably build some credibility through books. My personal dream was actually much bolder than that. I didn't want to just write a few books and serve a few clients. I wanted us to develop the framework of diversity management in much the same way that Abraham Maslow established the model of human needs fulfillment. I wanted to lead the way towards more open conversations about diversity. Anita and I thought a broader model would change the tone of the conversations, which it eventually did.

It was not smooth sailing by any means. We had months when the phone didn't ring but the rent checks were still due. We had clients who were forced to use us, either due to senior management directives or an occasional court order. In those cases, we would start in a hostile setting and usually be able to turn the group around and help them see the workshops as opportunities for growth. Those experiences left us emotionally and physically spent, and wondering what we got ourselves into.

The good news is that thirty-four years later, we have much to show. Depending on the day, I alternate between "shocking," "surprising," and "not there yet" as descriptors for our journey. While the firm of *Gardenswartz and Rowe* cannot claim the status of Abraham Maslow, we are the "go to" on diversity with a four-layer model that has become the gold standard. We recently published our tenth book, *Emotional Intelligence for Managing Results in a Diverse World*. We have won ample recognition, spoken around the world, and assisted clients in fostering a healthier work environment across industries, both corporate and non-profit.

Along the way, there have been some valuable lessons. I've learned, for example, that patience and persistence will usually rule the day even though we like to imagine a meteoric rise like we read about in the tabloids. The betting person should always opt for a "brick–by–brick" approach. We received that counsel early on from a successful philanthropist who told us, "Everyone wants their business to be shot out of a cannon and have instant success, but that is just not the way it happens." At the time, it was decidedly unsexy advice, but I have come to see it as the wisest advice we've ever received.

At seventy-one years of age, I am in the "giving back" mode more than ever. Being a septuagenarian may sound old but for many of us, but the combination of energy and perspective can still yield some amazing results. I am no longer worried when the phone doesn't ring because I know it will. I am still helping struggling groups, still facing the occasional recalcitrant participant, still receiving notes of thanks from individuals who tell us that the workshop's lessons extended to their lives on some personal level.

I pursued my passion right out of gate, and perhaps my biggest joy today is providing counsel to my nieces and nephews. They all seem to have a fire burning inside them, and "results" can't happen fast enough. They are part of an impatient generation that values speed too much for my liking. To them I say, "The path is long, the challenges are great, but if we can value the journey more than the endpoints, we may surprise ourselves." I know I have.

Once a Teacher,
Always a Teacher

Anita Rowe

Before I went to kindergarten I was lining up my dolls and playing teacher to them, so I knew early on my destiny was to be a teacher. It probably helped that in my generation there were three primary choices of professions for women: teacher, nurse, or secretary. My choice was also encouraged by my mother who counseled that teaching was an esteemed and secure profession, and would also enable me to be at home when my future children were growing up.

It was not surprising, then, that I earned my credential and began teaching junior high schoolers. I loved the job and took on a myriad of challenges ranging from setting up a reading lab to serving as faculty chairman. Just when I was starting to get bored, I was lucky enough to be selected for a special project to help the school district deal with court-mandated racial integration.

After three years of learning how to train adults and facilitate team building, my colleague Lee Gardenswartz and I decided to take a leap and start our own consulting business. I assuaged my guilt of leaving the school district by telling myself that I was still teaching, just in a different arena. While many of our friends and family commented on the financial risk of leaving the security of the school district for the unpredictable world of entrepreneurship, we felt the bigger risk was that of stagnating and not following our passion.

Slowly we began to build our client list; for two teachers who knew nothing about business except how to spell the word, it was tough going. We grabbed an opportunity when we read an article in the *Los Angeles Times* that featured a few groundbreaking women. We decided to talk to women who had "made it" to learn how to make our own business a success. What started as a few interviews grew to a much larger undertaking—meeting with one hundred of America's top professional women, including C suite members, elected officials, pioneers, and entrepreneurs. We began to identify key themes, those factors that were the heart of their successes. Before we knew it, our personal research project intended to help build our business turned into a book, *What It Takes: Good News from 100 of America's Top Business and Professional Women.*

But we had no publisher, and in the '80s self-publishing was not the option it is today. Not to be deterred, we contacted everyone we knew with connections in publishing and finally landed a publisher through the agent of one of our interviewees. By the time we went to New York to meet our agent, Doubleday (a publisher) was already lined up with an offer and a healthy advance. I remember crossing the street in Manhattan across from the Plaza

Hotel pinching myself to be sure I wasn't dreaming and saying to my business partner, "Pretty good for two teachers from Los Angeles Unified" (our school district). From there we went on to a whirlwind book tour, then to TV and radio interviews and book signings to launch the book.

Aside from the thrill of getting a book published, we learned formidable lessons from these one hundred women. We identified five factors that formed the foundation of their achievement. These powerhouses were *four-wheel driven*, inspired by challenge, change, freedom, and meaning. They loved their work ("Magnificent Obsession"), saw possibilities ("Megavision"), focused on performance and overcoming obstacles ("No Excuses, Just Results "), and built important sustainable relationships ("Practical Magic").

The journey with these women began our own transformation. I often noted that after completing these interviews, we would come home deflated. My husband would hear me wax poetic about the interviewee of the day and ask, "If they're so great, how come you're so down?" I realized we were comparing ourselves to these women's accomplishments and feeling like we hadn't done much.

Once we began to identify the factors that propelled their success, our feelings of inferiority changed. We could see that we also had developed those abilities in ourselves. Deflation turned into inspiration. We too had "what it takes." Even better, we were aware of what we needed to do to achieve our own goals. *What It Takes* became the first of many books, and to this day we continue to build our reputations, extend our consulting practice, and write on our topic of passion—how to create inclusion in the business world.

Like the women we'd interviewed, my career path turned out to be very different from what I'd expected—being a secondary teacher until retirement. Life has a way of surprising us. As it turned out I didn't have the children I'd anticipated. I never expected to be an entrepreneur building a consulting firm nor did I plan on getting a doctorate, or writing ten books. But, true to my original desire, I'm still a teacher, just in a different way.

When Four Becomes Eight

Anonymous

What do you do when you grow up with a mother whose great wish is that her daughter becomes a doctor? First you try to protest. Then when you finally become a doctor you understand the roots of her dreams. You see it as a mix of some projection, wanting the best for your daughter, and breaking down traditional barriers. It is not simply naked ambition.

Today I am eighty-two years old, a practicing psychiatrist and the champion of the slow and steady race. After I fulfilled my mother's dream, deciding that it really was my choice and not hers, I began the trip that has brought me to where I am today. There were starts and stops along the way. My residency took me eight years instead of four. Some would say nine if you count the year I took off while my husband went to New York for a training program. But I won the first heat of the race if it is measured in terms of becoming a practicing child psychiatrist. Add to my career that I was able to have a family of four kids, always trying to be there while they were growing up, along with a good marriage, and I feel I led the balanced life that I was striving for.

I entered Harvard Medical School in 1952 and was one of eight women in a class of about one hundred and sixty. I guess we were pioneers, and some were highly focused on proving that they could play in a man's world. As for me, my motivation was simply to help people, and medicine was a good way to do it.

It never occurred to me that my path was extraordinary. Although there were few of us in medical school, I had gone to Barnard and was accustomed to smart women wanting to achieve. But liberation only went so far. My friends were husband shopping while they hid their exceptional achievements, and they cautioned me, "You won't be able to hide the fact that you are going to Medical School." At the other extreme I was told I was trying to enter a man's world so I could more easily find a husband. We can now laugh at these quips, but back then our roles were clearly defined, and wife as physician was not one of them.

Two years into medical school, I met Sumner, a dentist, with whom I found many common interests. Only two months after we began dating, he was sent to far away places by the Navy. While I finished medical school, we wrote, kept the flame alive, and then when he returned, we married.

Shortly after my internship, we started our family. First I delivered twins and then before I knew it, I had three kids under the age of two! Three years later after the fourth was born, I wanted to resume my career. It was a challenge, yet I believed that if I were patient and steady, I would become the doctor I hoped to be. I knew I would need some flexibility and again by good fortune and a good choice, I found a program with a part-time track that allowed me to do a four-year residency in eight years. My colleagues accepted my needs and understood my plan of "slow and steady."

There were other good choices and fortune along the way. I chose child psychiatry over pediatrics because it would be easier to manage my schedule. I also made a good choice in marrying my husband. Sumner was a well-educated man who was proud that his wife was a physician. Adding to my good fortune, Sumner's widowed mother joined our household. She became the perfect childcare provider, combining loving grandmother with perfect baby-sitter. She saw the kids to school, made them put on a sweater when she was cold, and even figured out how to be watchful and discreet as they got older and needed their own space. During the years before residency, with my mother-in-law's help, I kept my skills alive by working a few afternoons a week at a city-run well-baby clinic in Boston. It had been suggested by a colleague who was in a similar position but was ready to move onto the next phase.

As time moved on, I completed my residency and saw my children grow into mature and productive teenagers. My first position post-residency was treating patients in the hospital. From there I proceeded to a mental health clinic and eventually joined a group of practitioners. Several years later the group disbanded, and I become a solo practitioner, which allowed me even more flexibility than before. Along the way other opportunities presented. At one point I considered a job as Dean of medical students, but as honored as I would be to be considered for the position, the job was full time and would not allow me to stay true to my goal of maintaining a balance between work and family.

I am frequently asked about retiring, and while I have considered it, I can never come up with a good reason why I should. I've made some changes that have allowed me to stay active professionally. I no longer see children; I find it difficult to get my aging body onto the floor, where I would often need to be when working with children. Also, the cases are often complex and at this point more than I want to take on. I continue seeing many of my older patients whose challenges I can identify with. I have also reduced my hours to meet my physical limitations. As always, I continue to value time spent with family. When grandchildren arrived more than twenty years ago, I felt it was important to give to my children what I got from my mother-in-law, and allotted several hours each week for childcare. Though the grandchildren are now grown, the importance of family I still hold dear. So with the changes I've made, the race goes on, sure and steady, and I'm enjoying every minute!

My Journey Into My Name

Peninnah Schram

"**N**o Ma! I won't move back to New London and live with you so I can take care of my children! I can't do that! I have to stay in New York and live my life with my children *here!*"

I don't know where I got the courage to take this stand at such a vulnerable and unexpected time of loss in my life. What had given me the *chutzpah* to make such a declaration? Had I even thought it through? How would I take care of two small children on my own?

My life had changed in an instant when one night my forty-two-year-old husband, and love of my life, died of a sudden heart attack. Those awful hours happened in slow motion as an out-of-body experience. At some point, I realized I had become a young widow at thirty-two. I kept repeating that unfamiliar word as if the mere sound would help me process my new reality.

When my mother offered for me to move to New London, CT so that my main responsibility would be to care for my toddlers (a three-and-a-half-year-old daughter and a fourteen-month-old son), I knew, intuitively, that was not a role I could accept. I needed to continue to choose life, not retreat. My identity as a woman, a professional, and a mother—although no longer a wife—had to be reconstructed, even if I didn't know how exactly. I knew that my mother's support would be important but in a less direct way.

Up to this time, my career had been running a small theatre company, "Theatre a la Carte", with a friend. At first, we produced one-act plays, and then we progressed to Jewish children's musicals, which we then toured around the tri-state area. It was immensely rewarding but offered little compensation.

Yet, just as we open the door for Elijah the Prophet at the Passover seder, I was blessed with a number of Elijah moments where doors were opened for me. The first door was opened by a college friend who chaired the Speech and Theatre Department at Iona College. He visited me during *shiva* (the Jewish week of mourning for my husband) and offered me an instructorship in his department. I spent that summer taking classes in preparation for being a teacher, and that fall was the beginning of a long career in college education.

In the spring of my first year of teaching, I was invited to a wedding of friends. I wanted to accept but cowered at the prospect of walking into a hall of couples dancing, when I felt so alone as a widow. I did an internal dialogue and reminded myself that it was a Jewish tradition and even responsibility to celebrate with the bride and groom. I accepted the invitation.

That night another door opened that changed my life. At the reception, I was introduced to the professor emeritus of Speech and Drama of Yeshiva University. We talked and, soon after, he phoned to offer me an interview with the Dean of Yeshiva College. After some starts and stops (mostly because I wasn't ready for more change), I accepted the offer to join the faculty at YU's Stern College. It was a fulfilling forty-five year stint of teaching at Stern College before I decided to retire last fall.

My story doesn't end there though. First I need to explain an issue I have wrestled with most of my life: my name. In the Book of Samuel, Peninnah is a very troubling figure. In the story of Samuel, she is one of two wives to Elkanah, the other being Hannah who is barren. While Hannah is loved more, Peninnah is fertile and has many children. In the story, Peninnah is the vilified wife as she taunts Hannah in a cruel and insensitive way.

I have often wondered why my father had chosen this name for me. What values was he celebrating? True, it was his mother's name, but it also says in the Jewish tradition that our names refer to a person's essence and have an influence on our life. Did he want me to become like Peninnah? Unkind? Unjust to others? This question occurred to me too late to ask my father.

One day, an epiphany struck me that allowed me to understand my father's decision. Peninnah means "pearl" in Hebrew. I discovered that a pearl is created through an irritant, a grain of sand. Only then are the luminous layers added on, one-by-one, to form this precious jewel. I suddenly realized that there was a positive role played by Peninnah as a catalyst in the biblical story. Peninnah causes Hannah a great deal of pain, but also becomes the reason that Hannah goes to the temple to pray with tears and a soundless prayer that came from the depths of her soul like never before. That was the prayer that God heard and opened Hannah's womb. Hannah became the mother of Samuel. This journey through my name opened a new door.

As I processed the "upside" of my name, I added to my identity and evolved into "Peninnah, the storyteller." This started when I volunteered to read books for The Jewish Braille Institute. This inspired me to tell stories beyond the recording studio. I contacted the Education Director at the 92nd Street Y to propose a storytelling program. Soon more doors opened. I was invited to be the Storyteller-in-Residence at The Jewish Museum. Then synagogues and conferences started inviting me as a storyteller. I became a champion of this art form and organized the Jewish Storytelling Network and Newsletter, wrote articles and books of Jewish folktales, and encouraged other storytellers. I had grown into my name.

Through the years, my mother remained my advisor, my anchor, my safety net, but I emerged as the independent strong-spirited woman that I had hoped to become back when I turned down her offer to move to New London. As for my children—they grew and prospered in their own way, but that is another story. I can look back at my journey, and my name, and feel proud. As a young widow, I couldn't imagine what lay ahead. But through some mix of faith, creativity, and practicality, Elijah's doors opened again and again, and an exciting future was forged.

Shameless Plugs

Allyson Straka, Mindful Nourishment LLC
Type of Business: Holistic Health Educators
Contact: www.Mindful-Nourishment.com,
allyson@mindful-nourishment.com

Alyson Ferranti
Ferranti Market Research & Consulting, LLC
Type of Business: Strategic Market Research
Contact: alysonferranti@gmail.com

Anita Rowe, Partner
Gardenswartz & Rowe, www.gardenswartzrowe.com
Type of Business: Consulting in Diversity and Emotional Intelligence
Contact: Emotional Intelligence and Diversity Institute,
www.eidi-results.org (310) 823-2466

Deborah Mead, poet
Book: *Topless*, co-authored by Deborah Mead,
Eileen McCluskey and Kara Provost
Available from MainStreetRag.com/bookstore

Donna Surges Tatum, PhD, CAE, CAEd
Meaningful Measurement, www.meaningfulmeasurement.com
Type of Business: Research and Psychometric Services.
Tools and techniques to enhance decision making.
Contact: donnatatum@meaningfulmeasurement.com

Evelyn Starr
E. Starr Associates, www.estarrassociates.com
Type of Business: Marketing and Brand Advisor, Writer, Speaker
Contact: evelyn@estarrassociates.com

Jeanette Kuvin Oren
Type of Business: Artist
Contact: www.KuvinOren.com jeanette@kuvinoren.com

Jill Kerner Schon
The Paint Bar
Type of Business: Paint-and-Sip Experience
Contact info: jill@thepaintbar.com

Judy Elkin
Judy Elkin Coaching, www.judyelkin.com
Type of Business: Mid-Career, Executive, and Parenting Coaching
Contact: judy@judyelkin.com

Kim Lorusso
Marketing Possibilities, LLC
Type of Business: Integrated Marketing Programs and Strategy
Contact: kimlorusso@mktgpossibilties.com

Laurel Mintz
Type of Business: Digital Strategy & Live Events
Contact: www.elevatemybrand.com, info@elevatemybrand.com

Lee Gardenswartz, Ph.D., Partner
Gardenswartz & Rowe, www.gardenswartzrowe.com
Type of Business: Consulting in Diversity and Emotional Intelligence
Contact: Emotional Intelligence and Diversity Institute,
www.eidi-results.org, (310) 823-2466

Lisa Pierson Weinberger, Esq.
Mom, Esq., www.momesquire.com
Type of Business: Employment Law Firm
Contact: lpw@momesquire.com

Melissa Ludtke
Touching Home in China: in search of missing girlhoods, touchinghomeinchina.com
Type of Business: Author, Digital Book Producer/publisher
Contact: Melissa.ludtke@gmail.com

Natalie Goldfein
My Habit Upgrade, www.nataliegoldfein.com
Type of Business: Personal Development & Self Improvement
System, Professional Coaching and Consulting
Contact: natalie@nataliegoldfein.com

Peninnah Schram
Interest: Jewish Storytelling and Jewish folktales
Books: *Jewish Stories of Love and Marriage: Folktales,*
Legends and Letters (co-author Sandy Sasso) to be published
October 2015 by Rowman and Littlefield
The Apple Tree's Discovery, published by Kar-Ben Publishing, 2012
Mitzvah Stories: Seeds for Inspiration and Learning,
Reclaiming Judaism Press, 2011.
Contact: peninnah1@aol.com

Ronna Benjamin
co-publisher (with Felice Shapiro) of www.betterafter50.com
Type of Business: online magazine for women 46-64
Contact: ronna@betterafter50.com

Sandy Serio Gregory
Che Bella Tours, www.chebellatours.com
Type of business: Small group tours offering good-life
experiences for culture seekers to savor and treasure
Contact: sandy.chebellatours@gmail.com

Susana Fonticoba
Right Click Advantage, www.rightclickadvantage.com
Type of Business: Digital marketing services, training, and
coaching, speaking engagements. Constant Contact Authorized
Local Expert and Master Certified Solution Provider
Contact info: 973-585-6393

Creating Your Piece

Creating Your *At My Pace* Piece

The following questions can help you get started creating your own piece:

Personal Story: Is there a story to share about you and your world that says a lot about who you are? Where you came from? Beliefs you hold dear? Family influences?

Key Moments: What are some major moments in the your journey? Did you change course, recommit and accelerate, hear an internal voice that altered your trajectory? Was there a u-turn or rest stop along the way? What purpose did any of these serve?

Ah-ha Discovery: In the course of your experiences, did you have a major discovery or identifying moment that shaped what you did next?

Looking Ahead: What do you wish going forward? See as your challenges? What strengths will you bring to manage those challenges?

Lessons Learned: What would you like to pass along to those looking for wisdom?

I've learned three helpful tips in working with women to craft their stories: avoid chronology, show don't tell, and don't be afraid to use humor. Above all, have fun with it. At the end of the day, the piece should be, to paraphrase the contributor Hillary Gardenswartz, a celebration of our choices.